# Develop an Affirmative Action Program as a Risk Management Tool

# Develop an Affirmative Action Program as a Risk Management Tool

*Dennis E Kaiser, SPHR*

iUniverse, Inc.
New York Lincoln Shanghai

**Develop an Affirmative Action Program as a Risk Management Tool**

iUniverse, Inc.

For information address:
iUniverse, Inc.
2021 Pine Lake Road, Suite 100
Lincoln, NE 68512
www.iuniverse.com


ISBN: 0-595-33663-9

Printed in the United States of America

I dedicate this book to my grandson Logan, the "Big Guy", who makes my life complete.

# CONTENTS

# Acknowledgments

---

I would like to thank those contractors who have afforded me the opportunity to work with them in developing their affirmative action programs. They have been my teachers in developing risk management through affirmative action.

I also thank my wife, Linda, whose support and understanding has been pivotal in making this book possible.

# PREFACE

---

Federal contractors are required to develop an affirmative action program and update that program annually. Unfortunately, a great deal of them do not gain the fullest value from that effort as once completed the "plan" goes on a bookshelf, collects dust, and isn't looked at until data is needed in order to update it.

Hopefully this book will change that mind set as the areas covered can have many uses in your people programs that will not only prevent litigations, but can improve morale, productivity, and even your safety record.

# WHAT AN AFFIRMATIVE ACTION PROGRAM IS

## (And What It Is Not)

I believe this brief Chapter is necessary due to the gross misconceptions of Affirmative Action that have been bantered around during recent years. Some are fiercely opposed to affirmative action as they contend they are against "quotas" at all costs. It's too bad they voice their opinions in that manner as they are simply indicating they oppose something they know very little about, because the regulations for Affirmative Action are also very opposed to "quotas", and it is so stated throughout the regulations. Some say they oppose "affirmative action" but favor "affirmative access", but when pressed to explain what "affirmative access" is they are silent and do not offer any definition. I believe "affirmative action" is nothing more than an organization's plan to ascertain whether they are treating people, all things being the same, as equal without regard to those things in life which a person has no control over such as race, color, sex, national origin, disability, and add to these religion and status as a protected veteran. The absence of age might be noted as while age discrimination is considered by the EEOC, it is not a consideration in affirmative action. Should this plan discover areas of potential "problems" it goes further and develops a course of action that will resolve those "problem areas", thus, it is a risk management tool that identifies areas that may become problematic if not rectified.

If this were a utopian society there would be no reason to have such regulations as equal employment opportunity and programs like affirmative action. However, we live in a society where people are selected, often times, not based on their qualifications, but on other considerations. How often has it been said, "It's not what you know, but who you know that matters?" Often times these "who you knows" are of the same race, religion, political party or have other similarities and not only can their hire eliminate a more qualified candidate, but can put an organization in a discrimination law suit. The point here is the selection decision had little or no bearing on qualifications, but on other factors. It is because of this "good old boy" system that still exists in our society that there needs to be some type of tool to assist those who have not had the opportunity to have their qualifications considered in the past, because they were not of the "right" race, color, sex, national origin, or religion.

An Affirmative Action Program is nothing more than a management tool designed to ensure equal employment opportunity. A central premise of affirmative action is that over time a contractor's workforce with reflect the gender, race, and ethnicity of the labor pools from which the contractor recruits and selects, providing there is no discrimination in the recruitment and selection process. An Affirmative Action Program contains a diagnostic component that includes a number of quantitative analyses designed to evaluate the composition of the workforce of the contractor and compare it to the composition of the relevant labor pools. There are also action—oriented programs that make up affirmative action programs. If the diagnostic components indicate that women and/or minorities are not being employed at a rate to be expected by the availability in the labor pool the contractor's program would then include specific steps, designed by the contractor, to address this situation. There are other components which go into an affirmative action program, and they will be discussed in subsequent Chapters of this book. Let it suffice for the nonce there are no "quotas", but simply opportunities for the contractor to look at, and evaluate, what is going on in its decisions regarding people. Even non-contractors might benefit greatly by looking at those same things within their workforce.

An Affirmative Action Program ensures equal employment opportunity by formalizing the contractor's commitment to equality in every aspect of the employment process. Affirmative action notwithstanding this is simply a sound business practice in keeping positive employee relations within the workforce. All employers should monitor and examine its employment decisions (hiring, promoting, terminating, training, etc.) and compensation system on at least an annual basis in order to evaluate the impact those systems have on all of their employees, not only women and minorities. Federal contractors in updating their affirmative action programs annually do this. Other organizations not being affirmative action employers, may not. An affirmative action-type program would do them well in risk management.

An Affirmative Action Program is more than a paperwork exercise. It includes those policies, practices, and procedures that the contractor implements to ensure that all qualified applicants and employees are receiving an equal opportunity for recruitment, selection, advancement, and every other privilege associated with employment. It should be a part of the way the contractor regularly conducts its business. When approached in this manner, I believe the employer's workforce will have a more positive morale than those organizations that do not examine such activities on a regular basis. The OFCCP also sees a more positive correlation between the presence of affirmative action and the absence of discrimination. Coincidence?

There are specific contents that must be included in all affirmative action programs and these will be discussed in detail in separate Chapters of this book, but will be mentioned here. As mentioned above, an affirmative action program includes a diagnostic component that includes quantitative analyses such as an Organizational Profile or Workforce Analysis, which examines your workforce by department or organizational unit; a Job Group Analysis, which examines your workforce by groupings of similar jobs; an Availability Analysis, which examines your recruiting labor pools for those people having requisite skills; and a Utilization Analysis, which compares your incumbency to the availability.

Other components required in your program are a designation of responsibility for implementation, which should be an individual who has authority to make changes and/or decisions relating to affirmative action; identification of problem areas; development of action—oriented programs; and periodic internal audits and reporting systems. A final requirement is that documentation be kept and made available to OFCCP on request.

# NOTES

# THE OFFICE OF FEDERAL CONTRACT COMPLIANCE PROGRAMS (OFCCP) AND AFFIRMATIVE ACTION

In 1965 President Lyndon B. Johnson signed Executive Order 11246. It was amended in 1967 by Executive Order 11375 and again in 1978 by Executive Order 12086. The Order prohibits discrimination by federal contractors on the basis of religion, sex, race, or national origin.

The Executive Order 11246 spells out the specific rules and regulations to be followed by contractors and subcontractors in Part 60—1. You should know and understand those rules and regulations and be able to identify and correct violations that may occur within your workplace.

On November 13, 2000 the OFCCP made revisions to Parts 60—1 and 60—2 of the Order and this book is based on those revisions. A complete copy of 41 CFR Parts 60-1 and 60-2 is located in the Appendices of this book.

The Office of Federal Contract Compliance Programs (OFCCP) is part of the U.S. Department of Labor's Employment Standards Administration (ESA) and has been given the authority to administer and enforce three equal employment opportunity laws that apply to Federal government contractors and subcontractors supplying goods and services to the Federal Government…It has a national network of six Regional Offices (New York City, Philadelphia, Atlanta, Chicago, Dallas, and San Francisco), each with District and Area Offices in major metropolitan centers. There are about 51 of these District Offices. A complete listing and contacting information of the district offices can be found in the Appendices.

The Office of Federal Contract Compliance Programs has been given the authority to enforce the following:

# Executive Order 11246

Prohibits discrimination and requires affirmative action to ensure equal employment opportunity without regard to race, color, sex, religion, and/or national origin.

<u>Who Must Develop An Affirmative Action Program?</u>

Those employers who are federal non-construction contractors or subcontractors, if:

- You have a federal contract of $50,000 or more, and 50 or more employees; or

- You have Government bills of laden which in any 12-month period, total or can reasonably be expected to total $50,000 or more; or

- Serves as a depository of Government funds in any amount; or

- Is a financial institution, which is an issuing, and paying agent for U.S. savings bonds and savings notes in any amount.

If you fall into any of the above examples, you are required to have a "written" affirmative action program for each of your establishments and you must require each non-construction subcontractor to develop and maintain a "written" affirmative action program for each of its establishments if it has 50 or more employees, even if that particular establishment does not have any federal contracts. If one establishment in an organization has a federal contract the entire organization must have a plan for each of the establishments having 50 or more employees. Should an establishment have fewer than 50 employees, you may choose to have a separate plan for that establishment or you may include them in the plan where management is directly involved.

When you meet the requirement for having a "written" affirmative action program you have 120 days from the commencement of a contract, or upon reaching the 50 employee criteria, to develop and implement your program. It then must be updated annually.

If you do not meet these criteria you are not required to have an affirmative action program. However, you can have one as a risk management tool as although you are not required to have a plan, you still are required to abide by equal employment opportunity laws set by the Equal Employment opportunity Commission (EEOC) and affirmative action plan have a proven track record of being.

It is not a coincidence that those organizations having an affirmative action program have fewer incidences of discrimination. As a risk management tool affirmative action works!

## Who is included in Affirmative Action Programs?

Contractors subject to the affirmative action program requirements must develop and maintain a "written" affirmative action programs for each of their establishments. Each employee in your workforce must be included in the affirmative action program of the establishment at which he or she works, with some exceptions. 1) Employees who work at establishments other than that of the manager, to whom they report, must be included in the affirmative action program of their manager. While this is easy enough to follow, the logic of it is not so clear. It is assuming their manager is the individual makes the employment decisions (hiring, wages, promotions, training, terminating, etc) therefore having the employee listed in that manager's plan can best measure that manager's decisions; 2) Employees who work at an establishment where the contractor employees fewer than 50 employees may be included under any of the following options: a) in an affirmative action program that covers just that establishment; b) in the affirmative action program that covers the location of the personnel function which supports the establishment; or, c) in the affirmative action program that covers the location of the official to whom they report. 3) Employees for whom selection decisions are made at a higher-level establishment within the organization must be included in the affirmative action program of the establishment where the selection decision is made. 4) If a contractor wishes to establish an affirmative action program other than by establishment, the contractor may reach agreement with OFCCP on the development and use of such a program based on functional or business units. The Deputy Assistant Secretary must approve such agreements.

If you have employees included in an affirmative action program other than where they are located you must be able to identify them. In such cases the Workforce Analysis/Organizational Profile and the Job Group Analysis of the affirmative action program in which the employee is included must be annotated to identify the actual location of such employee. If the establishment at which the employee actually is located maintains an affirmative action program, the Workforce Analysis/Organizational Profile of that program must be annotated to identify the program in which the employee is included.

We shall discuss these "includes" and "excludes" later in more detail.

## Section 503 of the Rehabilitation Act of 1973, as amended

Prohibits discrimination and requires affirmative action in all personnel practices for qualified individuals with disabilities. It applies to all firms that have a nonexempt Government contract or subcontract in excess of $10,000. An affirmative action program is required.

1.  Covers government contractors and subcontractors.
2.  Mandates affirmative action to employ and advance in employment otherwise qualified disabled persons.
3.  "Otherwise qualified" means capable of performing the "essential functions" of the job sought or desired with or without a "reasonable accommodation."
4.  Has implementing regulations that require some covered contractors to have a "written" Affirmative Action Program which may be inspected by applicants and employees.
5.  OFCCP issued new regulations on May 21, 1996 which were effective August 29, 1996. Primary purpose was to conform to ADA regulations. Other major changes affecting AAPs and employment practices are to shift mandatory invitation to self-identify from pre-offer to post-offer, pre-employment. This is not to be confused with the self-identify you

will need for your applicant flow information, to be discussed later; it simply means you cannot ask if there is a disability before you make a job offer.

6.  Remedies and penalties are the same as the Executive Order.

## 38 USC 4212—The Vietnam Era Veterans' Readjustment Assistance Act of 1974 (VEVRAA)

This prohibits discrimination and requires affirmative action in all personnel practices for special disabled veterans, Vietnam Era veterans, and veterans who served on active duty during a war or in a campaign or expedition for which a campaign badge has been authorized. It applies to all firms that have a nonexempt Government contract or subcontract of $25,000 or more. An affirmative action program is required.

1.  Covers government contractors and subcontractors.
2.  Mandates affirmative action to employ and advance in employment "otherwise qualified" disabled veterans and veterans of Vietnam Era.
3.  **Requires that the employer list all jobs with the state employment service <u>except</u> 1) "executive and top management", 2) positions that will be filled from within the contractor's organization (including affiliates and other locations), and 3) jobs lasting three days or less.** You can list your jobs through America's Job Bank on the Internet. To get to that website you can go through our site at http://h-r-m-s.com.
4.  Has implementing regulations that require some covered contractors to have a "written" Affirmative Action Program <u>which may be inspected by applicants and employees</u>.
5.  Related regulations require the annual filing by September 30th of the VETS—100 Report.
6.  OFCCP need no complaint to trigger a compliance review.
7.  Remedies and penalties are the same as outlined in Executive Order 11246.

There are a few exceptions as to who is covered by these regulations. Those limitations are listed below:

1.  Contracts involving work performed outside the United States—Under executive Order 11246, such contracts are exempt from coverage if the

employees performing the work were not recruited within this country. Section 503 and VEVRAA apply only to "employment activities within the United States," which is defined as including actual employment within the United States and decisions of the contractor made with in the United States pertaining to employees and applicants who are within the United States, regarding employment activities abroad.

2.　Contracts with State or Local governments—An agency, instrumentally or subdivision of a State or local government is not subject to the requirements of the EEO clause unless it participates in work on or under the contract.

3.　Contracts with certain educational institutions—Religiously oriented church-related colleges and universities may hire employees of a particular religion without violating Executive Order 11246.

4.　Contract involving work on or near an Indian reservation—contractors are permitted to extend a preference in employment to Indians for work performed on or near an Indian reservation.

The Deputy Assistant Secretary for OFCCP may grant exemptions for specific contracts or categories of contracts for national security reasons. Exemptions also may be granted for facilities not connected with the Government contract. You may apply for an exemption through your local OFCCP office.

## OFCCP Responsibilities

There are several ways the OFCCP carries out its regulatory and enforcement responsibilities. In fact, we have found the agency to be one of the most cooperative government agencies in lending itself to help contractors.

Among those responsibilities of the OFCCP are:

1.　Offering technical assistance to Federal contractors and subcontractors to help them understand regulatory requirements and the compliance evaluation process. We have found the Columbus, Ohio District Office to be most helpful in offering not only their expertise, but their time as well.

2. Conducting compliance evaluations and complaint investigations of Federal contractors' and subcontractors' personnel policies and practices.

3. The agency has the responsibility of assisting contractors and subcontractors in forming linkages between them and the Department of Labor's employment and training programs, outside organizations and recruitment sources to help employers identify and recruit qualified employees.

4. When necessary, the OFCCP will negotiate agreements, including formal Conciliation Agreements, with contractors and subcontractors found in violation of regulatory requirements.

5. After a Conciliation Agreement has been placed in effect the agency has the responsibility of monitoring the progress of the contractor or subcontractor in fulfilling the terms of that agreement. This is usually accomplished through having the contractor or subcontractor submit periodic compliance reports.

6. The most drastic responsibility of the OFCCP is recommending enforcement actions to the Solicitor of Labor. Typically this does not occur unless the contractor or subcontractor is out of compliance and is doing little or nothing to meet the regulations.

The OFCCP also shares enforcement responsibilities with other Federal agencies in the administration of the following laws:

- **Title VII of the Civil Rights Act of 1964, as amended**, which prohibits employment discrimination by employees with 15 or more employees on the basis of race, color, national origin, sex, and religion. In many instances, employment discrimination claims against a contractor can be brought under both Executive Order 11246 and Title VII. In April of 1999 the OFCCP was given the authorization to act as the Equal Employment Opportunity Commission's (EEOC) agent in processing, investigating and resolving the Title VII component of complaints filed with OFCCP under executive Order 11246 that allege discrimination of a systemic or class nature on the basis of race, color, national origin, sex, or religion.

- **Title I of the American's with Disabilities Act of 1990 (ADA)**, which prohibits employment discrimination by employers with 15 or more employees against qualified individuals with disabilities. Again, the EEOC has the primary authority for enforcing the ADA but OFCCP is authorized to act as EEOC's agent in processing and investigating ADA complaints falling within the overlapping jurisdiction of Section 503 and title I of the ADA.

- **Immigration Reform and Control Act of 1986 (IRCA)**, which requires employers to maintain I-9 Forms for the U.S. Immigration and Naturalization Service which verify their employees' eligibility to work in the U.S.

## Responsibilities of the Contractor

Although the remainder of this book will cover how to meet the responsibilities of the contractor and subcontractor of federal contracts, it may be helpful to summarize briefly what those responsibilities are. Contractors and subcontractors are required to not discriminate against any employee or applicant and to take the affirmative action to ensure that applicants and employees are treated without regard to race, color, religion, sex, national origin, disability, or status as a protected veteran.

All of those activities requiring a selection decision are considered in determining whether the contractor is meeting its responsibility. Among those selection decisions would be those which involve employment, rates or pay or other compensation, fringe benefits, promotions, upgrades, recruitment, selection for training, transfers, layoffs, returns to work from layoff, demotions, and any other instance where a selection decision must be made.

In addition to those selection decisions are several other responsibilities contractors and subcontractors have. Among these is in the solicitations for employees the contractor must state that all qualified applicants will receive consideration for employment without regard to race, color, religion, national origin, disability, or status as a protected veteran. This is typically done by placing the tagline "EEO/M/F/D/V" in all printed advertisements.

The contractor must post in a conspicuous place a notice indicating employees and applicants of the contractor's position on equal employment opportunity, affirmative action for Women and Minorities, and affirmative action for Disabled and Veterans. It must also state the AAP for Disabled and Veterans is viewable to those applicants and employees wishing to view it. The contractor should state, in the posting the time and place this document can be examined. Sample postings are offered in the Appendices.

The contractor must comply with personnel record retention requirements which are published in 41 CFR 60—1.12, 60—250.80, and 60—741.80.

The contractor must comply with the Uniform Guidelines on Employee Selection Procedures, which are published in 41 CFR Part 60—3 as well as with the guidelines on discrimination because of religion or national origin, which are published at 41 CFR Part 60—50.
Other responsibilities of the contractor and subcontractor include the submission of the EEO—1 Report and the VETS—100 both of which are due annually on September 30th.

## How Does the OFCCP Investigate?

In carrying out its responsibilities, the OFCCP uses the following enforcement procedures as specified in Executive Order 11246 Part 60—1, Subpart B:

### Compliance Reviews

A Compliance Review, the most "popular" of the mechanism employed by the OFCCP, is a comprehensive analysis and evaluation of a contractor's hiring and employment practices, "written" affirmative action plan, and result of affirmative action efforts. There are three stages of a Compliance Review:

- Desk Audit—this is when the Compliance Officer will request specific information to be reviewed prior to their coming to the establishment being reviewed. The Desk Audit gives the Compliance Officer the opportunity to review the contractor's basic organizational structure, examine the contractor's personnel policies and procedures, and identify areas where there has been a lack of progress in meeting goals and the information that will be needed to evaluate the contractor's good faith efforts. They will examine the contractor's development and implementation of action-oriented programs, who is responsible for what, what internal mechanisms are in place to identify problem areas, and what internal auditing and reporting systems are in place and how effective they appear to be. This will also give the Compliance Officer an opportunity to identify areas of potential discrimination where minorities and women are underrepresented and concentrated in the workforce, where employment activity has been disadvantageous to women and minorities, and where there may be problems in the compensation of women and minorities. This latter area is one of chief concentration at the time this book is "written". Due in part to limited personnel, the OFCCP is ending more and more reviews at this point, not going on-site. This in itself should be an encouragement for organizations to have "letter-perfect" "written" plans and documentation.

- On-Site Investigation—this segment of the Compliance Review is done on the contractor's premises. This portion of the review may last from several hours to several days. It will begin with an opening conference with the CEO where the OFCCP's mission and the compliance evaluation process are discussed. After this entrance conference the Compliance Officer will begin to compare the data and information reviewed during the Desk Audit with the actual employment practices at the company. Other items you might expect the Compliance Officer to review personnel, pay and other employment records. You might expect to have employees and other company officials to be interviewed by the Compliance Officer, get employee files to be reviewed, or any information the Compliance Officer questions as a result of the Desk Audit. An exit conference with the CEO is generally held on the last day of the on-site. If that is not possible the Compliance Officer may schedule a time to return for the exit conference. Typically, a good indicator to what the Compliance Officer may choose to investigate more fully would be those areas they request further information during the Desk Review process. They will typically call your EEO/AA Coordinator requesting further documentation and information. It is extremely important to take copious notes of their requests in order to ascertain the direction their review may go once they come on site.

- Off-Site Analysis—the Compliance Officer now analyzes the entire information gather during the Desk Audit and the On-Site Investigation and makes an initial determination as to whether the contractor's policies and procedures comply with OFCCP regulations.

- Notice of Findings—this is the final phase of the review. The OFCCP will notify the contractor of the findings of the review. If there are no problems or violations noted, the contractor will be so advised with a Notice of Review Completion. If problems or violations do exist, the OFCCP will issue the contractor 1) a Pre-Determination Notice outlining issues and allowing for contractor responses, and/or 2) a Notice of Violations, containing an explanation of the violation(s) found, recommendations for corrective action and suggested ways to improve the contractor's EEO and affirmative action performance record.

All Compliance evaluations, with the exception of the Compliance Check, will begin with the scheduling of a full-scale compliance review. In most cases, the results of the Desk Audit will determine whether an on-site review is warranted. The compliance evaluation may close at the end of the Desk Audit or can continue with an on-site investigation that involves an examination of several issues or may be focused on one or two issues.

The data the OFCCP will request, as outlined in their letter to your organization, is as follows:

A.    "A copy of your Executive Order Affirmative Action Program (AAP) prepared according to the requirements of 41 CFR 60-1.40 and 60-2.1 through 60-2.17". The specific items are as follows:

1.  An Organizational Profile prepared according to 41 CFR 60-2.11

2.  The formation of job groups (covering all jobs) consistent with criteria given in 41 CFR 60-2.12

3.  For each job group, a statement of the percentage of minority and female incumbents, as described in 41 CFR 60-2.13

4.  For each job group, a determination of minority and female availability that considers the factors given in 41 CFR 60-2.14(c)(1) and (2)

5.  For each job group, the comparison of incumbency to availability, as explained in 41 CFR 60-2.15

6.  Placement goals for each job group in which the percentage of minorities or women employed is less than would be reasonably expected given their availability, consistent with 41 CFR 60-2.16

B.  A copy of your Section 503/38 U.S.C. 4212 AAP9s) prepared according to the requirements of, respectively, 41 CFR Parts 60-741 and 60-250. (These are your AAP(s) for Veterans and Disabled Veterans, and Disabled Workers)

C.  The support data specified in the Itemized Listing, as follows:

7.  A copy of your Employer Information Report EEO-1 for the last three (3) years.

8.  A copy of your collective bargaining agreement(s), if applicable. Please also include any other information you have already prepared that would assist us in understanding your employee mobility (promotions, etc.) system(s).

9.  Information on your affirmative action goals for the preceding AAP year and, where applicable, progress on your goals for the current AAP year. See 41 CFR 60-1.12(b), -2.1(c) and -2.16

    This must include information that reflects a) job group representation at the start of the AAP year (i.e., total incumbents, total minority incumbents, and total female incumbents) b) the percentage placement rates (% goals) established for minorities and/or women at the start of the AAP year; and, c) the actual number of placements (hires plus promotions) made during the AAP year into each job group with goals (i.e., total placements, total minority placements, and total female placements). For goals not attained, describe the specific good faith efforts made to achieve them.

10. Data on your employment activity (applicants, hires, promotions, and terminations) for the preceding AAP year and, if your are six months or more into your current AAP year when you receive this listing, for the current AAP year. This data must be presented either by job group (as defined in your AAP) or by job titles (41 CFR 60-3.14 and 3.15)

11. Please provide annualized compensation data (wages, salaries, commissions, and bonuses) by salary range, rate, grade, or level showing total number of employees by race and gender and total compensation by race and gender. Present these data in the manner most consistent with your current compensation system.

This request will be contained within a letter (See Appendix A). You should check the OMB Number to be assured it is valid. You are not required to respond to an outdated OMB Number. While it is a simple thing for the OFCCP to obtain a valid Number, it does indicate to them you are aware of your rights and are perceptive.

You can be assured that the compliance officer will request additional information during the desk audit stage of the review, and most certainly you will be required to produce further files and/or documents during the on-site evaluation.

## Compliance Checks

This is a relatively new method implemented by the OFCCP to ascertain whether a contractor has maintained records consistent with the requirements, developed an AAP, and is working toward equal employment. While this review may well be passé at this time due to the EO Survey, it may still be used; therefore it will be discussed briefly here.

This is typically initiated by a telephone call or fax, then a letter, giving the contractor 3 to 5 business days to prepare for an on-site visit.

This letter will list those pieces of data they will be evaluating while on-site, typically the following:

1. A report of results under you prior year's Affirmative Action Program; (a summary of your goals (see #9 above)

2. Examples of job advertisements, including listing with state employment services; and

3. Examples of accommodations made for persons with disabilities.

4. Your EEO-1 Reports for the past three years
This on-site visit should take no longer than twenty minutes.

## Pre-Award Review

This is a review conducted when an award in excess of $10 million is awarded and will typically review contract information and race and gender of workforce on those contracts.

A phone call will normally initiate this type of review and may, or may not be followed up by a letter or fax. You will be requested to send the compliance officer specified material pertaining to your previous/present contracts along with the race and gender mix.

## Corporate Management Reviews ("Glass Ceiling Review")

These are not specifically authorized as a separate type of review in the regulations. They involve larger private contractors and the purpose is to ascertain whether individuals are encountering artificial barriers to advancement into mid-level and senior corporate management.

These are quite lengthy and detailed with the compliance officer(s) often times taking "residence" within the facility while the review is conducted. During reviews of this nature special attention is given to those components of the employment process that affect advancement into mid and senior level positions. Also, a great deal of attention is paid to compensatory matters.

This type of review is becoming more popular and can include outside "establishments" of the contractor, not just the headquarters, as in the past. If, during the course of an investigation, it comes to the attention of OFCCP that problems exist at establishments outside the corporate headquarters, OFCCP may expand the compliance evaluation beyond the headquarters establishment. At the discretion of OFCCP it may direct its attention to and request relevant information for any and all areas within the corporation to ensure compliance with Executive Order 11246.

<u>Complaint Review</u>

These are initiated as the result of a complaint that has been filed and will generally be focused on the area of the complaint. This may result in a "Focused Review" which consists of an on-site review restricted to one or more components of the contractor's organization or one or more aspects of the contractor's employment practices.

# The OFCCP's System for Selecting Contractors for Review

The newly created Equal Opportunity Survey (aka EO Survey) is the instrument that will be the primary "triggering" mechanism used by the OFCCP to initiate further inspection of a contractor's affirmative action program. A full chapter in this book is devoted to this survey in hopes you will become familiar with it and learn the extreme importance of it.

As of July 2004 the OFCCP replaced the Equal Employment Data System (EEDS) that had been used for years to determine which establishments would be reviewed with the Federal Contractor Selection System (FCSS).

**How does OFCCP select contractors for compliance reviews under the new OFCCP selection system?**

OFCCP selects a subset of contractor establishments that submitted an EEO-1 report to receive a compliance review, traditionally selecting between 2,000 and 4,000 establishments per fiscal year. Beginning in July, 2004, OFCCP implemented a new selection system, called the Federal Contractor Selection System (FCSS), to better target compliance reviews based on an indication of potential workplace discrimination. The new system is based on external research conducted by Westat, a firm recognized for their expertise in data collection and analysis. Unlike prior OFCCP systems that were developed internally by OFCCP without the benefit of a systematic study, the new system draws upon Westat's thorough analysis of data from 10 years of OFCCP compliance reviews to formally identify and characterize relationships between reported EEO-1 workforce profiles and findings of discrimination. The Westat study developed a mathematical model that predicted the likelihood of a finding of systemic discrimination (defined as compliance review that resulted in a conciliation agreement in the amount of $100,000 or more between 1995 to 2000). OFCCP's Division of Statistical Analysis further refined the Westat model to incorporate recently released Census data. The FCSS model involves seventeen factors that compare the workforce profile of the establishment to those of establishments in the same industry classification and to that of the local labor market using 2000 Census data.

To select the establishments for compliance reviews for the current FCSS cycle, the OFCCP began by utilizing the list of contractors submitting EEO-1 reports for 2002. From this list, the OFCCP excluded some establishments for selection based on a variety of criteria, including, for example, establishments that completed a review within the last two years, were involved in an open review as of March 2004, were part of a FAAP agreement, or submitted an EO survey in 2004. After making these exclusions, we used the FCSS model to rank the establishments based on their estimated likelihood of a systemic discrimination finding. From this ranking, OFCCP selected about 3,500 establishments of the top-ranked establishments for possible compliance reviews during this cycle. We also imposed a set of constraints to ensure that we do not impose an excessive burden on multiple establishment contractors. Furthermore, under the new system, the OFCCP attempted to better identify whether a potential contractor actually holds a current federal contract by matching the EEO-1 list to a commercial database of federal contracts.

Contractors should note that while the mathematical model developed does assign a higher likelihood of discrimination to some establishments than others, and that this measure was used to make the selections, the accuracy of this model has yet to be tested; a test is underway as part of the initial scheduling.

Furthermore, while the model develops an individual establishment measure, such measures are far too inaccurate to conclude that discrimination exists in a particular establishment. The strength of such measures rests in their use in an aggregate setting to separate a large group of establishments with higher values from those with lower ones, which only on average, we expect to have greater need for a compliance review. Given the inaccuracy of the individual results, and the conclusions that could be drawn from it, OFCCP does not plan to release the specific model parameters to enable contractors to replicate such a measure for their establishments.

**How does OFCCP plan to schedule the reviews among the selected contractors?**

OFCCP is conducting the scheduling in rounds. In the first round, which began in July 2004, we released a list of approximately 650 establishments to receive scheduling letters. OFCCP created this subset of the 3,500 selections to serve as a pilot study by taking the subset of these cases with the highest likelihood measures to validate the effectiveness of the new selection system. No additional scheduling is planned until the desk audit phase of these pilot reviews is completed. Once that occurs, OFCCP will release the remaining selections in rounds based on the work requirements in the local offices.

In response to contractor concerns about simultaneous scheduling of multiple reviews for a given contractor, we also designed the new system so that no more than three establishments from the same corporation (subject to the accuracy of the corporate establishment linkages provided on the EEO-1 data) are scheduled in the same round. Note: We did not impose such a restriction to create the pilot listing; some corporations may receive more than three establishment reviews during the pilot round of compliance reviews.

Given a late development of the new system in fiscal year 2004, OFCCP plans to schedule all or some portion of the 3,560 selections from this cycle well into fiscal year 2005 or until the scheduling of all of the 3,560 selections or some subset is completed. OFCCP may elect not to schedule all of the 3,560 cases based on the results of the pilot evaluation. In any case, at this time we expect little or no new scheduling beyond these 3,560 selections to occur before the spring of 2005.

**How many reviews could my corporation receive during this cycle?**

Also in response to contractor concerns, in forming the set of 3,560 selections we designed the system so that in this cycle, each corporation (again as limited by the parent corporation identification numbers on the EEO-1 reports) would receive no more than 25 compliance reviews between July 2004 and the end of the cycle (potentially spring 2005 as discussed above). Since under the old system, scheduling occurred on a relatively fast pace during the spring of 2004, we decided to offer additional relief to reduce the compliance review count by subtracting from the maximum count of 25 the number of reviews the corporation had open as of March 2004. For example, if a corporation had 16 reviews open as of March 2004, we would only schedule up to nine new ones for this cycle. We note that even with these restrictions, a contractor could receive more than 25 reviews in the last 12 months. Contractors that consider the number of reviews over the last calendar year to be excessive should contact the OFCCP National Office. Based on the near term frequency of reviews conducted and ongoing, OFCCP may elect to close some subset of the reviews scheduled currently as part of a scheduling agreement.

A third "trigger" would be a complaint filed by a group or an individual.

## What are the OFCCP's Enforcement Procedures?

Immediately upon finding that a contractor either has no affirmative action program, has deviated substantially from an approved affirmative action program, or has failed to develop or implement an affirmative action program that complies with the regulations, that fact will be recorded in the investigation file. Typically, whenever administrative enforcement is contemplated the notice to the contractor will be issued giving the contractor 30 days to show cause why enforcement proceedings under section 209(a) of Executive Order 11246, as amended, should not be instituted. The notice to show cause should contain:

- An itemization of the sections of the Executive Order and of the regulations with which the contractor has been found in apparent violation, and a summary of the conditions, practices, facts, or circumstances which give rise to each apparent violation;

- The corrective actions necessary to achieve compliance or, as may be appropriate, the concepts and principles of an acceptable remedy and/or the corrective action results anticipated;

- A request for a "written" response to the findings, including commitments to corrective action or the presentation of opposing facts and evidence; and

- A suggest date for the conciliation conference.

Should the contractor fail to show good cause for its failure or fails to remedy that failure by developing and implementing an acceptable affirmative action program within 30 days, the case file shall be processed for enforcement proceedings pursuant to Section 60—1.26. If an administrative complaint is filed, the contractor shall have 20 days to request a hearing. If a request for hearing is not received within the 20 days from the filing of the administrative complaint the matter will proceed in accordance with Part 60—30 of the regulations.

During the "show cause" period of 30 days, every effort will be made through conciliation, mediation, and persuasion to resolve the deficiencies which led to the determination of non-responsibility. If satisfactory adjustments designed to bring the contractor into compliance are not concluded, the case shall be processed for enforcement proceedings pursuant to Section 60—1.26 which might have the case referred to the Department of Justice where the Attorney General may bring a civil action in the appropriate district court of the United States requesting a temporary restraining order, preliminary or permanent injunction, and an order for such additional equitable relief, including back pay, deemed necessary or appropriate to ensure the full enjoyment of the rights secured by the order.

As a result of the above-mentioned reviews and investigations the OFCCP has the following enforcement procedures authorized:

- Obtains Letters of Commitment and Conciliation Agreements from contractors and subcontractors who are in violation of regulatory requirements.

- Monitors contractors and subcontractors progress in fulfilling the terms of their agreements through periodic compliance reports.

- Forms linkage agreements between contractors and Labor Department job training programs to help employers identify and recruit qualified workers.

- Offers technical assistance to federal contractors and subcontractors to help them understand the regulatory requirements and review process.

- Recommends enforcement actions to the Solicitor of Labor.

- The ultimate sanction for violations is debarment—the loss of a company's federal contracts. Other forms of relief to victims of discrimination may also be available, including back pay for lost wages.

The OFCCP has close working relationships with other Departmental agencies, such as: the Department of Justice, the Equal Employment Opportunity Commission and the Department of Labor, the Office of the Solicitor, which advises on ethical, legal, and enforcement issues; the Women's Bureau, which emphasized the needs of working women; the Bureau of Apprenticeship and Training, which establishes policies to promote equal opportunities in recruitment and selection of apprentices; and, the Employment and Training Administration, which administers Labor Department job training programs for current workforce needs.

# NOTES

# Overview of Contractor Obligations

## §Part 60-1

All covered federal contractors are required to not discriminate against any employee or applicant and to take affirmative action to ensure that applicants and employees are treated without regard to race, color, sex, national origin, disability, or veteran status.

The activities covered are those in which a contractor has the opportunity to make an employment decision such as: rates of pay or other compensation, fringe benefits, promotions, recruitment, selection for training, transfers, layoffs, returns from layoff, demotions, hiring, and any other type of decision that might occur regarding a person's standing within your organization.

In addition to the selection decisions a contractor also has other obligations, as indicated:

## Record Retention

Any personnel or employment record developed or maintained by the contractor must be retained for a period of not less two years from the date the record was made or the personnel action involved, whichever occurred later. If you have fewer than 150 employees or do not have a government contract of at least $150,000 the minimum retention period is one year from the date of making the record or the personnel action involved, whichever is the later. These records include, but are not limited to, records pertaining to hiring, assignment, promotion, demotion, transfer, lay off or termination, rates of pay or other terms of compensation, and selection for training or apprenticeship, and any other records having to do with requests for reasonable accommodation, the results of any physical examination, job advertisements and postings, applications and resumes, tests and test results, and interview notes. In the case of involuntary termination of an employee, the personnel records of the individual terminated would also be included in this regulation.

Other items that would be retained under these regulations would be any notice received by the contractor notifying a complaint of discrimination had been filed, that a compliance evaluation has been initiated, or that an enforcement action has been commenced. All records relevant to the complaint must be preserved, including compliance evaluation or enforcement action until final disposition of the complaint, compliance evaluation or enforcement action.

According to the regulations 60—1.12(a) the term "personnel records relevant to the complaint" would include "personnel or employment records relating to the complainant and to all other employees holding positions similar to that held or sought by the complainant and application forms or test papers submitted by unsuccessful applicants and by all other candidates for the same position as that for which the complainant unsuccessfully applied." Where a compliance evaluation has been initiated, all personnel and employment records are relevant until the OFCCP makes a final disposition of the evaluation.

For any record you maintain you must be able to identify the gender, race, and ethnicity of each employee and, where possible the gender, race, and ethnicity of each applicant. This information must be supplied to the OFCCP upon their request.

Failure to preserve these records will constitute noncompliance in regard to your obligations under the Executive Order. If you have destroyed, lost, or failed to retain records as required by the Order, there will most likely be a presumption that the information destroyed, lost or not retained would have been unfavorable to you. The only circumstance where this would presume such an unfavorable assumption might be where the destruction or loss was due to circumstances outside of your control.

## Other Obligations

In all employment advertising the contractor must state that all qualified applicants will receive consideration without regard to race, color, religion, sex, national origin, disability, or veteran status. Typically, the tagline "EEO/M/F/D/V" is sufficient for satisfying this requirement.

If there is a collective bargaining agreement between the contractor and its employees the contractor must notify the labor unions or other representative(s) of the employees advising them of the contractor's commitments to ensuring that applicants and employees are treated without regard to race, color, sex, religion, national origin, disability, or protected veteran status. Displaying a notice in a conspicuous place that is visible to employees and applicants can usually satisfy this responsibility. An example of such notice can be found in the Appendix.

The contractor must comply with the Uniform Guidelines on Employee Selection Procedures that are published at 41 CFR Part 60—3.

The contractor must comply with guidelines on discrimination because of religion or national origin. These are published at 41 CFR Part 60—50.

# NOTES

# ORGANIZATIONAL PROFILE
# OR
# WORKFORCE ANALYSIS

## The Organizational Profile (§60-2.11)

An organizational profile is a depiction of the staffing pattern within an establishment. It is one method contractors use to determine whether barriers to equal employment opportunity exist in the organization. It provides an overview of the workforce at the establishment that may assist in identifying organizational units where women or minorities are underrepresented or concentrated. The contractor has a choice of using the Organizational Display or the Workforce Analysis, discussed below.

## The Organizational Display (§60-2.11(b)

Among the additions to the regulations proposed by the OFCCP is that of the Organizational Profile. This profile is an organization depiction of the staffing patterns within an establishment and will be presented in a format showing the organizational units/departments, the title of the person in charge of that particular unit, and the gender and race of that individual. This is followed by the total number of employees in that unit and a breakdown by gender and race (see diagram.) Although we presented this information in chart form it need not be in this particular format. This format was used simply to show the information required by the regulations. You may choose to display the information in detailed graphical or tabular chart, text, spreadsheet, or any similar presentation

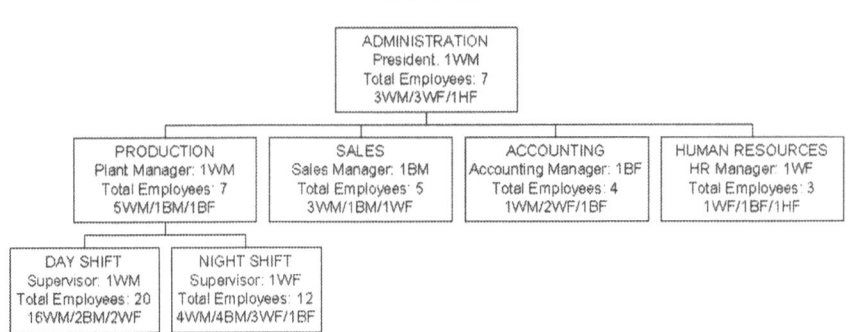

as long as the information required is included in your display. (A sample Organizational Display follows):

## Organizational Display
## XYZ Company (1/1/2005)

| Organizational Unit Supv's Race/Sex, Title | Total | Total Min | Females | | | | | | Males | | | | | |
|---|---|---|---|---|---|---|---|---|---|---|---|---|---|---|
| | | | T | W | B | H | A | I | T | W | B | H | A | I |
| Management WM, President | 5 | 1 | 1 | 1 | 0 | 0 | 0 | 0 | 4 | 3 | 1 | 0 | 0 | 0 |
| Office BF, Office Mgr | 6 | 2 | 6 | 4 | 1 | 1 | 0 | 0 | 0 | 0 | 0 | 0 | 0 | 0 |
| Production WM, Shop Mgr | 51 | 14 | 17 | 10 | 3 | 2 | 1 | 1 | 34 | 27 | 2 | 5 | 0 | 0 |
| Facility Total | 62 | 17 | 24 | 15 | 4 | 3 | 1 | 1 | 38 | 30 | 3 | 5 | 0 | 0 |

The OFCCP believes this type of display will provide a representation the establishment into organization units which will indicate of where minorities and women may be underrepresented or concentrated. The OFCCP defines "organizational unit" as any component that is part of the contractor's corporate structure. In the more traditional organization, an organizational unit might be a department, division, section, branch, group, or similar component. In a less traditional organization, an organizational unit might be a project team, job family, or similar component.

It is the OFCCP's contention this profile display would eliminate the paperwork necessary in doing a Workforce Analysis and, therefore, relieve the contractor of much time in developing.

In reality, however, although this format appears to simplify the process, it is believed to actually add time to its completion, as most of the information must be actually formatted by the contractor, as software to extract this information from HRIS systems is void at the present time.

An Organizational Display is also not conducive to the structure of many companies as they are quite fluid, project teams disappear as the project ends, and such a chart could soon become outdated. Our experience proves it difficult to determine who the actual "manager" of a unit is due to the structure of an organization. It is also a concern that much information might result in the loss of valuable compliance information that is included in the Workforce Analysis. In looking at the sample profile above one can see it is quite simple in it construction, however, it is also void of much information that is included in the Workforce Analysis.

One area a contractor might be cautioned of is the potential of the connecting lines to be misinterpreted by the OFCCP compliance officer as "Lines of Progression." You should be aware of, and indicate your lines of progression in order to show promotional avenues within your establishment.

In determining your lines of progression you should use discretion. You might consider the following guidelines in preparing this report:

- List natural lines of progression. For example, Date Entry Operator can promote to Senior Data Entry Operator.

- List historical lines of progression. For example, Clerk can promote to Clerk typist, can promote to Secretary.

- One job can be included in more than one line of progression.

- Do not list unusual promotions as progressions. For example, Secretary can promote to Supervisor.

- Positions that have no progression within a functional unit should be listed as having no progression. For example, the Manager in a department/organizational unit would have no line of progression within that unit.

If your organization has an open and well-utilized internal job posting practice, you may not have any clearly defined lines of progression. If this is the case a listing of career ladders may be included in this section rather than specific progression reports. Where lines of progression can play a major role is in promotions. If the OFCCP feels a certain job leads to another, and you have a promotion that doesn't follow that line and a woman or minority appeared to be by-passed, they may contend this was due to discrimination. So, beware of the lines of progression.

## The Workforce Analysis (§60-2.11(c))

The Workforce Analysis does more, in my opinion, than the Organizational Profile. It is a listing of each job title as it appears in any applicable collective bargaining agreements or payroll records ranked from the lowest paid to the highest paid within each department or other similar organizational unit. It summarizes employees by Department or Unit and job title. No individual employees are listed on reports although you might consider organizing your data by use of employee name in order to crosscheck as you go. You do not include the names in your final report, but I have found it is much easier to locate omissions or additions that may occur in processing job titles. The Workforce Analysis calculates race and sex counts by job title within each department (how many white males, white females, black males, etc.) You will note that job titles are necessary, where they were not required in the Organizational Profile. It is our belief this makes it easier to analyze just who makes up each particular department/unit. It also orders job titles within department by compensation from lowest to highest paid. With more emphasis on compensatory practices, it is believed the Workforce Analysis allows the contractor one other "look" at compensation practices within your establishment.

A sample format for the Workforce Analysis might look something like:

XYZ COMPANY
Workforce Analysis
January 1, 2005

Department: Production

| EEO | JOB TITLE | SALARY | TOT EMP | M T | A W | L B | E H | A | I | F T | E W | M B | A H | L A | E I | TOT MIN |
|---|---|---|---|---|---|---|---|---|---|---|---|---|---|---|---|---|
| 5 | Warehouse Worker | 7.50–8.75 | 20 | 10 | 4 | 2 | 2 | 1 | 1 | 10 | 9 | 1 | 0 | 0 | 0 | 7 |
| 5 | Machinist | 10.00–14.00 | 30 | 23 | 17 | 1 | 5 | 0 | 0 | 7 | 6 | 1 | 0 | 0 | 0 | 7 |
| 1 | Shop Manager | 60000 | 1 | 1 | 1 | 0 | 0 | 0 | 0 | 0 | 0 | 0 | 0 | 0 | 0 | 0 |
| | TOTAL | | 51 | 34 | 22 | 3 | 7 | 1 | 1 | 17 | 15 | 2 | 0 | 0 | 0 | 14 |

The contractor will complete a similar chart for each of its departments/organizational units. While it appears the Workforce Analysis is more work, one must remember that you will be using the same data you compile for the Job Group Analysis. Plus, I believe, the Workforce Analysis provides you with more evaluative information and that is the purpose of doing this in the first place. It gives the job titles which can better allow you to evaluate each particular unit in terms of what is actually being performed in that unit. It provides you with compensation data not included in the Organizational Display. The Workforce Analysis will uncover discrepancies in pay arrangements. For example, a common problem is discovered where some in a job title are paid as an "Exempt" while others are paid as "Non-Exempt". The Organizational Display will not reveal such "problems".

You should also give details regarding your lines of progression much the same as was discussed previously.

The contractor has the option of utilizing either of these displays in meeting the requirements of the regulations. You must determine which one will allow you the most beneficial data.

# NOTES

# JOB GROUP ANALYSIS (§60-2.12)

The Job Group Analysis is probably the most important analysis you will make in the development of your AAP. The revised regulations makes it required that you include it in your plan. If your job groups are inappropriately composed, your availability and utilization analyses will be flawed as they are based on these groups. The regulations give you a great deal of latitude in developing job groups and should take extra time on arranging your groups.

The Job Group Analysis is the first step in comparing the representation of minorities and women in your workforce with the estimated availability of qualified minorities and women who could be employed. A Job Group Analysis combines job titles within your establishment. Although you do not have to list your employees by name, you might want to gather the information using names in order to keep better tracking of your incumbents.

A Job Group is a grouping of job titles that share similar wages, content, and opportunities. Contractors are given considerable discretion in determining which jobs to combine, but they should contain those requisite common elements. Similarity of content refers to the duties and responsibilities of the job titles that make up the job group. Similarity of opportunities refers to training, transfers, promotions, pay, mobility, and other careers enhancement opportunities offered within the job group.

In developing Job Groups, it is easier if you break the task into two steps; 1) Categorize each job title at your company into one of ten EEO Job Categories as defined below, and 2) After you have sorted all of the Job Titles into one of the ten EEO Job Categories, you analyze job titles a second time and break them

36

down further by those with similar wage rates, job content and promotional opportunities.

**Step 1.** Categorizing each Job Title into one of the ten specific job categories defined by the Federal government.

## EEO Job Categories

(1) **Officials and Managers**—Occupations requiring administrative and managerial personnel who set broad policies, exercise overall responsibility for execution of these policies, and direct individual departments or special phases of a firm's operations. Includes: officials, executives, middle management, plant managers, department managers, and superintendents, salaried supervisors who are members of managements, purchasing agents and buyers, railroad conductors and yard masters, ship captains and mates (except fishing boats), farm operators and managers, and kindred workers.

(2) **Professional**—Occupations requiring either college graduation or experience of such kind and amount as to provide a comparable background. Includes: accountants, auditors, airplane pilots, and navigators, architects, artists, chemists, designers, dieticians, editors, engineers, lawyers, librarians, mathematicians, natural scientists, registered professional nurses, personnel and labor relations specialists, physical scientists, physicians, social scientists, teachers, and kindred workers.

(3) **Technicians**—Occupations requiring a combination of basic scientific knowledge and manual skill which can be obtained through about 2 years of post high school education, such as offered in many technical institutes and junior colleges, or through equivalent on the job training. Includes: computer programmers and operators, drafters, engineering aides, junior engineers, mathematical aides, licensed, practical or vocational nurses, photographers, radio operators, scientific assistants, surveyors, technical illustrators, technicians, and kindred workers.

(4) **Sales**—Occupations engaging wholly or primarily in direct selling. Includes: advertising agents and salesworkers, insurance agents and

brokers, real estate agents and brokers, stock and bond salesworkers, demonstrators, salesworkers and sales clerks, grocery clerks and cashier checkers, and kindred workers.

(5) **Office and Clerical**—Includes all clerical type work regardless of level of difficulty, where the activities are predominantly nonmanual though some manual work not directly involved with altering or transporting the products is included. Includes: bookkeepers, cashiers, collectors, messengers and office helpers, office machine operators, shipping and receiving clerks, stenographers, typists and secretaries, telegraph and telephone operators, legal assistants, and kindred workers.

(6) **Craft Workers (Skilled)**—Manual workers of relatively high skill level having a thorough and comprehensive knowledge of the processes involved in their work. Exercise considerable independent judgment and usually receive an extensive period of training. Includes: the building trades, hourly paid supervisors and lead operators who are not members of management, mechanics and repairers, skilled machining occupations, compositors and typesetters, electricians, engravers, job setters (metal), motion picture projectionists, pattern and model makers, stationary engineers, tailors and tailoresses, arts occupations, handpainters, coaters, and kindred workers.

(7) **Operatives (Semiskilled)**—Workers who operate machine or processing equipment or perform other factory type duties of intermediate skill level, which can be mastered in a few weeks and requires only limited training. Includes: apprentices, operatives, chauffeurs, delivery workers, dryers, furnace workers, laundry and process workers, stationary firefighters, truck and tractor drivers, weavers, welders and flamecutters, electrical and electronic equipment assemblers, butchers and meatcutters, inspectors, testers and graders, handpackers and packagers, and kindred workers.

(8) **Laborers (Unskilled)**—Workers in manual occupations which generally require no special training perform elementary duties that may be learned in a few days and require the application of little or no independent judgment. Includes: garage laborers, car washers and greasers,

gardeners (except farm), and groundskeepers, stevedores, wood chop-
pers, laborers performing lifting, digging, mixing, loading and pulling
operations, and kindred workers.

(9) **Service Workers**—Workers in both protective and non-protective service occupations. Includes: attendants (hospital and other institutions,
professional and personal services, including nurses aides and orderlies),
barbers, charworkers and cleaners, cooks (except household), counter
and fountain workers, elevator operators, firefighters and fire protection,
guards, doorkeepers, stewards, janitors, police officers and detectives,
protectors, waiters and waitresses, amusement and recreations facilities
attendants, guides, ushers, public transportation attendants, and kindred workers.

(10) **On—The—Job—Trainees:**
**Production**—Persons engaged in formal training for craft-workers when
not trained under apprentice programs—operative, laborer, and service
occupations.
**White Collar**—Persons engaged in formal training for official, managerial,
professional, technical, sales, office and clerical occupations.

**Step 2.** After you have sorted all of the Job titles into one of the ten EEO Job
Categories, you then break them down further by those with similar wage rates,
job content and promotional opportunities. For example, you may have determined the following jobs fall into EEO Job Category (1) Officials and Managers
according to the definitions listed above:

> President & CEO
> Vice President, Operations
> Vice President, Human Resources
> Engineering Manager
> Plant Manager
> Vice President, Finance
> Maintenance Manager
> Sales Manager
> Supervisor (12)

Looking at the definition of Job Group of similar content, similar wages, and similar opportunity you note that all is not similar in the list of jobs listed above. Content similarity, where "content" relates to the duties of the job usually means the technical "know-how" required for the position. Therefore, while the President & CEO and the Plant Manager may have the technical "know-how" required for their position, they do not manage at the same level; therefore putting them in the same job group may not be warranted. The same might be true for the Plant Manager and Supervisors. Using this example, therefore, you might have three Job Groups within this EEO Job Category, as follows:

101 Top Management
        President & CEO
        Vice President, Operations
        Vice President, Human Resources
        Vice President, Finance

102 Middle Management
        Plant Manager
        Maintenance Manager
        Engineering Manager
        Sales Manager

103 Lower Management
        Supervisor

You would then go through the other nine EEO Job Categories and break job titles into those with similar content, wage rates, and promotional opportunities. Keep in mind that similar wage rates should not be an overriding factor in the determination of job groups. In fact, content and opportunity may be considered as more important. Consider the level of technical "know-how" required, the ability to take advantage of training opportunities, transfers, promotions, mobility to desirable wage and/or salary situations and other employments before considering wage rates.

Keep in mind this example was for purposes of indicating varying differences among jobs within the EEO Job Categories. If this were an actual company you might consider keeping all of these job titles together in one Job Group in order to not have many smaller groups. Remember, the regulations allow contractors of fewer than 150 employees to form Job Groups by EEO Category.

Another essential of the Job Group Analysis is that it calculates race and sex counts by job title within each job group.

Finally, your Job Group Analysis orders job titles by compensation from lowest to highest paid. As with the Work Force Analysis, an evaluation of the pay ranges can reveal potential "problems" that can be corrected internally before external sources get involved. A glance at the compensation ranges may also reveal a job title that may be misplaced in a given job group.

Your Job Group Analysis would look similar to the following diagram:

## XYZ COMPANY

### Job Group Analysis

**JOB GROUP: 501 CLERICAL SUPPORT**     **DATE: January 1, 2005**

| JOB TITLE | COMPENSATION | M | F | B | H | A | I |
|---|---|---|---|---|---|---|---|
| Receptionist | 7.50 -8.25 | | 2 | | | | |
| Admin. Assistant | 9.25 – 9.75 | | 1 | 1 | | | |
| Payroll Administrator | 10.25 | 1 | | | | | |
| Executive Secretary | 11.75 | | 1 | | | 1 | |
| TOTAL | | 1 | 4 | 1 | 0 | 1 | 0 |

We might have this broken further, by indicating the number of Males by race and of Females by race and that is a good practice as information required for the Equal Opportunity Survey, to be discussed in another chapter, will require you to have such information and we believe you should streamline your efforts as much as possible, overlapping information where you can. This will not only make it easier for you, but will also assure you are not contradicting your information.

Now that we have discussed what a Job Group is and what it does let's look at what information you will need in order to put your job groups together.

This is one reason we advocate the use of the Workforce Analysis, discussed in the previous Chapter, is the same information is needed for both analyses. Again, that information is as follows:

- Employee Name
- Job title
- EEO Code
- Department/Organizational Unit
- Annualized Compensation
- Gender
- Race
- Job Group
- Date of Hire
- Corporate Initiative

The employee names are not essential, in fact should not be listed when submitting your data in the Job Group Analysis, however having the names can prove very helpful in tracking information as you proceed. It is not rare to get to tallying up your job groups to find that the numbers do not "come out". Having the names of employees can better help you to pin point who may have been left out, or counted twice.

Other information you might include would be the residence of each employee or at least the city or county they reside in plus their zip code. Although this information is not necessary for your Job Group Analysis, it may be helpful in determining your recruitment areas for each job group.

The date of hire is not required in the regulations either, however we include it as the compensation analyses required for Part "C" of the EO Survey. We find it more efficient to gather this information all at one time, especially if our HRIS is able to extract it. Other dates that should be tracked are in addition to the date of hire, the date the individual employee started their present job, and the date the employee started in their present pay grade. These will allow you to do a much more thorough compensation analysis.

These groups can be formed in one of two methods, geographical or functional. The geographical is the most common as it simply groups all employees at a given establishment into job groups. Some larger organizations, however, find it more meaningful to group employees by the "function" of their job, regardless of where they are located. Under such a grouping all members within such a functional grouping would be calculated in the availability and utilization analyses for the establishment of where their manager resides. In order to use the functional method you must gain approval. Whichever method you use you must make sure each of your employees is counted. Functional AAPs will be discussed later in this book.

Because job groups are used in calculating Availability and Utilization it is essential that much diligence be taken in forming them. We will discuss Availability and Utilization more fully in the next chapter, but suffice it to say at this point that we should strive to make our job groups as large as possible in order they be more statistically significant. It is for that reason, the OFCCP allows those contractors with fewer than 150 employees to use the EEO Code in forming job groups.

As mentioned previously, job groups tend to coincide with EEO Job Categories. This being true makes it important to avoid some of the common mistakes in assigning EEO—1 Categories.

## Common Mistakes in Assigning EEO—1 Categories

1.  **Inflated Job Titles Lead to Errors in EEO—1 Codes**

    The root to many mistakes made in assigning job titles to EEO—1 Report Categories is in the job titles themselves. Employers often use job titles that are misleading about job content—typically inflating the title vis a vis the size of the job. This happens most often with "management" titles and with high-level clerical/administrative titles.

    For example, an employer may have a job title of "Accounts Payable Coordinator" to which they have assigned the EEO—1 Code for "Officials and Managers" when the content of the position is clearly clerical. Or the job title "Project Engineer" may be associated with a job that genuinely set broad policies, exercises overall responsibility for execution of these policies, and directs individual departments or special phases of the operation, or, it may simply be the title of an engineer who herself reports to an engineering manager.

2.  **Assigning Hourly Paid or Non-Exempt Supervisors the EEO—1 Category Code for Officials and Managers or Craft Workers.**

This is undoubtedly the most common error of all. **First level supervisors must be classified along with those employees under their supervision.** The loading Dock supervisor is an "8"; the supervisor for Truck Drivers is a "7", the Office Manager is a "5", and the Foreman of the Mechanic Shop is a "6". **None** of these positions are properly classified as "Officials and Managers", "1", check your AAP; there's a good chance that's where they've been reported.

3.  **The EEO—1 "Coder" has No Special Competence in the Area nor Ultimate Use for the Data S/He is Coding.**

A common mistake is to give the job of assigning EEO—1 Codes to a clerk in the Human Resource office or—worse—to individual department heads. Only the EEO Officer should have the authority to assign or to change EEO—1 Category Codes! Only this person understands the implications for reporting as well as for AAP Job Group Analysis purposes.

4.  **Permitting "Politics" to Influence Coding**

Although this is, perhaps, not a "common" mistake it occurs often enough to bear mentioning. Particularly in banks or research organizations where titles are strongly associated with both status and educational accomplishments (though not necessarily compensation), we have seen situations where clerical people insisted that their EEO—1 Category be designated as "2", or "Professional".

Some companies even go so far as to allow employees to determine whether they would be classified as "exempt" or "non-exempt"!

5. **Assuming that if you have "Semi-Skilled" Workers, you must also have "Skilled" Workers**

   Not infrequently are operative positions been coded as "6" or "Craft Workers" simply because they were the highest paid of all production workers. Not so. Read the definitions. Similarly, your entry-level workers may not be "Unskilled" simply because they are your lowest level employee if the job content requires skills and experience beyond that acquired in a few days.

**Keep in mind that the regulations do not specify what you must use for job groups other than stating they should be of similar wages, content, and opportunity. You should also attempt at making your job groups as large, in numbers, as possible in order to ensure more accurate statistical analyses. For best results, it would be preferred to have job groups no smaller than 30 people.**

While developing your job groups it is important to maintain copious notes so you can not only document what you are doing in making your job group determinations, but it will also prove extremely beneficial should you be audited and questioned by the OFCCP. These notes will also prove valuable in completing next year's AAP.

Finally, remember the importance of developing your job groups, take extra time and "pain" in doing so. Your efforts and diligence will be rewarded in the end.

# NOTES

## JOB GROUP WORKSHEET

| EEO | JOB TITLES | PAY RANGE | CONTENT | OPPORTUNITY |
|-----|-----------|-----------|---------|-------------|
| 1 | | | | |
| 2 | | | | |
| 3 | | | | |
| 4 | | | | |
| 5 | | | | |
| 6 | | | | |
| 7 | | | | |
| 8 | | | | |

# NUMERICAL ANALYSES

## The Availability Analysis (§60-2.14)

The next step in your analysis is the Two Factor Analysis which requires that you consider two different factors in deciding whether or not a particular job group is underutilized with females or minorities. For those of you who are reading this as a "refresher", this was once called the 8 Factor Analysis, but the OFCCP revised it to 2 factors, an External Factor, which is the geographical area from which you usually seek or reasonably could seek workers to fill the positions in a particular job group, and an Internal Factor, which are those employees you have who are promotable, transferable, or trainable. As in the past, the contractor is given the discretion of whether a factor is pertinent to a given Job Group, however be able to explain why a factor you chose not to use was not relevant to that job group.

The availability must be determined for each job group for women and for minorities. In other words you will go through each job group and calculate the availability for women, and then you will go through each job group and calculate the availability for minorities.

To calculate the availability for the External Factor you will need to examine each job group in order to ascertain where you actually recruit when you have an opportunity. This will, most likely, vary from job group to job group. For example, when you have an open requisition for a Vice President of Finance you might place an advertisement in the Wall Street Journal, let's assume nationally. But, when you have an open requisition for a Machinist you might advertise in the local newspaper. This information might indicate your recruitment area for those positions. Past experience might also be an indicator as to where your employees come from. The results of your examination would give a pretty good indication of where the external recruitment area is for each job group.

Once you have determined where you recruit you could obtain census data from your State Employment Office. While they will provide this information free of charge be aware it will usually break the jobs down only as far as EEO Listings (Officials and Managers, Professionals, Technicians, etc.). Therefore, you may want to purchase a specific census run detailing the information for your company from one of the companies such as HR Management Solutions, LLC and you can get the information from the internet (http://h-r-m-s.com) or your local library. Be aware that beginning January 2005 the 2000 Census will be used in determining your availability.

The importance of obtaining the most detailed census data you can is so you can more accurately match your jobs with those having the requisite skills in your recruitment area. If, for example you have Electrical Engineers a more detailed census would enable you to get the number of Electrical Engineers available in your recruitment area. Using the information from your State Employment Office might only give you the number of Professionals, which would not only have the Electrical Engineers, but also the accountants, teachers, and all other professionals in your recruitment area. So you can see the significance of gaining the most precise census data you can in order to be as precise as possible in calculating the availability statistics.

Once you have obtained and recorded the information for the External Factor for each Job Group you next would examine each group in order to see whether the Internal Factor is pertinent. In order for you to ascertain whether the Internal Factor is pertinent you will need an in-depth picture of how your internal positions are filled. The most accurate way of obtaining this picture is to list each employee within a job and trace their background within your company from one job group to another position in a new group…This method is referred to as the Historic Method. While this is a time consuming project it does let you gain a good knowledge of your actual progressions or "Feeder Groups" which can help a great deal in developing an accurate Affirmative Action Plan. It can also be helpful in your career counseling efforts.

Another method, the Discretionary Method, allows a potentially more informed method of calculating feeder or career growth information since it involves listing groups of employees by position title, race and sex who might be promoted to positions in each job group, if any, to determine internal availability. Using this method you would examine each of your groups to consider where in your organization you might look if you had to fill a position. For example, should you need to replace a floor supervisor you might look to your skilled workers or your semi-skilled workers. These groups would then be your feeder groups, assuming your supervisors are in a job group different from skilled and/or semi-skilled workers. Such an evaluation might be documented as indicated on the following:

### XYZ COMPANY
### Feeder Groups for Promotions
### (Internal Factor)

| JOB GROUP | TOTAL EMPLOYEES | % WOMEN | % MINORITIES |
|---|---|---|---|
| 101–Executives<br>The highest positions in Job Group 102 | 10 | 20% | 10% |
| 102–Middle Management<br>Job Groups 201 and 202 | 20 | 5% | 10% |
| 201–Technical Professional<br>Job Group 301 | 15 | 20% | 26.7% |
| 202–Non-Technical Professionals<br>No internal promotions to this group | 0 | 0% | 0% |
| 301–Technicians<br>No internal promotions to this group | 0 | 0% | 0% |

By utilizing one of these two methods, for minorities and for women, for each job group, you will have considered the Internal Factor in your analysis and that is what the regulations require. In the example above you would use the Internal Factor when calculating availability for Job Groups 101, 102, and 201, but not for Job Groups 202 and 301 and this is okay because you did consider the factor for those two Job Groups.

In determining your internal factor also gives you the opportunity to evaluate your employee base for those individuals who might have the potential to move up your organizational "ladder". Identifying these individuals can assist you in "targeting" positions they are qualified to move into, possibly with additional training which you can plan to give them. This planning in itself can control turn-over of those employees you would best be served by not losing.

You have now examined your job groups to see where you fill the positions that make them up, both, internally and externally. You must do one more thing before calculating the availability for each group and that is to determine the significance each factor has in filling each of your Job Groups. While not actually required by OFCCP you might want to put a weight on each factor to identify the importance each has in filling your groups. For example, if you have a group which is comprised of ½ the people coming from external sources and ½ coming from internal promotions; you would give each factor a weight of 50% for a total of 100%. You would use any proportions as your examination of each group would indicate. For those groups in which you didn't use one of the factors the weighting would be 100% and 0% for a total of 100%.

# NOTES

## Worksheet for Tracking Potential Promotions

| Job Group | Employee, Job Group, Job Title (considered within this year) | Minority% | Female% |
|---|---|---|---|
|  |  |  |  |
|  |  |  |  |
|  |  |  |  |
|  |  |  |  |
|  |  |  |  |
|  |  |  |  |
|  |  |  |  |

## Incumbency v. Estimated Availability (§60-2.15)

This analysis is actually nothing more than comparing your incumbency to the availability within your recruitment pools, your external and internal sources, in each job group. When the percentages of minorities or women employed in a particular job group is less than what would be reasonably expected given their availability percentage in that particular job group, the contractor must establish a placement goal. Placement goals will be discussed more fully at another point.

In determining whether a placement goal must be established there are several "rules" which can be elected by the contractor. You can choose between the Any Difference Rule, which simply indicates a placement goal is established if the incumbency is simply less than the availability percentage. The second rule is the "80% Rule", which indicates a placement goal is to be established if the incumbency is less than 80% of the availability percentage. A third rule is the "Two Standard Deviation Rule", which indicates a placement goal is warranted if the incumbency is less than two standard deviations of the availability.

A process we would recommend would be what might be called a "progressive process." By this I mean you would first look at a Job Group's current Utilization for Women and Minorities, as shown in the example below:

Step 1—Current Incumbency for Job Group: ___Engineers_____
Total Incumbents in the Job Group: ___100___

| | | | |
|---|---|---|---|
| Total Women: | 20 | Total Minorities: | 10 |
| Percent Women: | 20.0% | Percent Minorities: | 10.0% |
| Availability Women: | 34.5% | Availability Minorities: | 12.5% |

Step 2—"Expected Participation" (Compute only if actual is *less* than availability)
Availability of Women % x Total Incumbents          34.5 "Expected"
Availability of Minorities % x Total Incumbents      12.5 "Expected"

Step 3—Compute Discrepancy
Expected Participation of Women (Step 2)             34.5
Minus Actual Participation of Women (Step1)          20
                                                     14.5 Discrepancy

Expected Participation of Minorities (Step 2)        12.5

Minus Actual Participation of Minorities (Step1)          10

                                                        2.5  Discrepancy

Step 4—"The Whole Person Rule"
Is the discrepancy for Women *at least one whole person?* (.999999 is <u>not</u> 1.0)
Women: Yes __X_ No _____
Is the discrepancy for Minorities *at least one whole person?*
Minorities: Yes __X__ No ____
**If the answer is "No", you need go no further. There is no underutilization
and no Placement Goal need be established. If the answer is "Yes", proceed to
Step 5.** In this case we need to proceed for Women as the discrepancy of 14.5 is
greater than a whole person. We also need to proceed for Minorities as the discrepancy of 2.5 is greater than a whole person.

Step 5—Computing Underutilization
Again, this is only necessary when the discrepancy equal at least one whole
person (Step 4). You may choose any "appropriate" rule for measuring whether
the discrepancy is so large as to be "unreasonable". The OFCCP has not issued
"written" guidance on determining "appropriateness". You may choose any true
test for statistical significance—standard deviation analysis is one that has been
approved by the Courts. Generally, the OFCCP prefers that standard deviation
not be used to measure underutilization in small groups (usually less than 30
incumbents), and we agree in that smaller groups would not give a statistically
significant result. The OFCCP generally prefers the use of their so-called "80%
Rule", which is <u>not</u> a true test for statistical significance. For illustrative purposes
we will use both of these "rules".

## The 80% Rule

Multiply the Availability of Women % by .80          27.6%
Multiply the Availability of Minorities % by .80          10.0%
Compare this answer with the actual participation %. If the <u>actual</u> is **greater**
than 80% of availability, no underutilization. If it is less, you must declare underutilization and set a Placement Goal.

## Standard Deviation Analysis

1.    Compute the size of the Standard Deviation:
Take the square root of:
(incumbents x availability of women (or minorities)) x (100% minus availability %)
*(HINT: Convert % to a decimal; don't forget to perform the functions inside the parentheses before multiplying the two; take the square root **last**).*

      Size of Standard Deviation for Women:    __2.13__

      Size of Standard Deviation for Minorities: __1.04__


2.    Compute the Number of Standard Deviations
Divide the Discrepancy (Step 3) by the Size of the Standard Deviation, above.

      Size of Standard Deviations for Women    __6.81__

      Size of Standard Deviations for Minorities __0.42__

If the number of Standard Deviations is 2 or more, you must declare underutilization and set a Placement Goal.

Step 6—Declaration of Underutilization and Placement Goals


Underutilization for Women? __Yes__ If "Yes", set a Placement Goal equal to the Availability of women. The Placement Goal for this AAP Year is to fill __34.5%__ of vacancies with women.

Underutilization for Minorities? __No__ No need to set a Placement Goal.

# PLACEMENT GOALS (§60-2.16)

Placement Goals serve as objectives or targets reasonably attainable by means of applying every good faith effort to make all aspects of the entire affirmative action program work. They are also used to measure progress toward achieving the ultimate target—equal employment opportunity.

While it is actually "written" in the regulations that a determination that a Placement Goal is required, it is not an admission by the contractor that discrimination has taken place. When writing your narrative, however, I recommend you clearly state this same.

Where it is deemed necessary to establish a Placement Goal for a particular Job Group, that goal must be at least equal to the availability figured derived for that particular group (women or minorities). It is also understood that goal is for that AAP Plan Year and would represent the target percentage of hires for that group in the current year. For example, if you are required to establish a Placement Goal of 30.0% for Women engineers and you actually hired a total of 100 engineers during the year, to attain your goal you should have hired at least 30 Women.

The establishing of Placement Goals for Minorities will include all minorities. In the event of a substantial disparity in the utilization of a particular minority group, the OFCCP may require the contractor to establish a separate Placement Goal for that particular minority group.

In establishing placement goals, the following principles apply (taken directly from the regulations, §60-2.16

1.   Placement Goals may not be rigid and inflexible quotas, which must be met, nor are they to be considered as either a ceiling or a floor for the employment of particular groups. Quotas are expressly forbidden.

2.   In all employment decisions, the contractor must make selections in a nondiscriminatory manner. Placement Goals do not provide the contractor with a justification to extend a preference to any individuals, select an individual, or adversely affect an individual's employment status, on the basis of that person's race, color, religion, sex, or national origin.

3.   Placement Goals do not create set-asides for specific groups, nor are they intended to achieve proportional representation or equal results.

4.   Placement Goals may not be used to supersede merit selection principles. Affirmative action programs prescribed by the regulations in this part do not require a contractor to hire a person who lacks qualifications to perform the job successfully, or hire a less qualified one.

5.   A contractor extending a publicly announced preference for American Indians as is authorized in 41 CFR 60—1.5(a)(6) may reflect in its placement goals the permissive employment preference for American Indians living on or near an Indian reservation.

# NOTES

# DISCRIMINATION ANALYSES

Contractors with 100 or more employees must maintain and have available for each job records and other information showing the impact of the combined effect of all selection procedures leading to the final employment decision by identifiable race, sex and ethnic groups. At least annually, contractors of 100 or more employees are required to analyze these decisions to determine whether the total selection process for each job is having adverse impact. The Uniform Guidelines defines "adverse impact" as "a substantially different rate of selection of hiring, promotion, or other employment decision which works to the disadvantage of members of a race, gender, or ethnic group." At the time of this writing race/ethnic groups are; Black or African American, Hispanic, Asian/Pacific Islander, American Indian/Alaskan Native, and White. Effective January 2005 the following will be: Black or African American, Asian, Native Hawaiian or Pacific Islander, American Indian or Alaskan Native, White, and Hispanic or Latino. The EO Survey asks for this break out at this time although they will allow you to use the former for the moment. Best advice would be to begin collecting information on your employees and applicants in the later descriptions.

As is true in each of the previously mentioned analyses, counting the right numbers is essential in conducting adverse impact analyses. Whereas the other evaluations examine potential problem areas in your program that may require additional action-oriented efforts to remedy, these evaluations may well disclose discrimination, and that can be extremely costly.

The selection processes to be evaluated are your hires, promoted, and terminated during the past AAP Year and we shall discuss them separately because there are specific things to be evaluated in each of these operations.

# Offers of Employment

Some call this process "Hires", and often misrepresent their actual activity, to their disadvantage, by not reporting those they "offered" an employment opportunity to, but for some reason did not end up being employed. "Offers" are, in fact, a positive decision made in your process. Therefore, they should be counted as a "positive." If you do not reflect them as a positive, they automatically become a rejection, and will count against you in the final calculations.

In evaluating your hiring selection process you have to consider two things: 1) who were the **applicants**; and, 2) what was the decision made with each of those applicants?

First, let's look at the ever debated question of "**Who is an Applicant?**"
The question has arisen, "Who is an applicant?" because when people had to appear in person and fill out a job application form, it was fairly clear who an applicant was. Now, with Internet tools like auto responders, broadcast capability and so forth, individuals are able to submit their names to companies even if they don't look at a job requisition announcement. So, there is a substantial increase in unsolicited resumes today. Companies are receiving thousands of submissions today compared to a small fraction of that amount in the past.

The Uniform Guidelines make it clear that "applicants" as a group are the foundation of all statistical analysis in disparate impact testing. If you aren't sure how to identify an applicant, it makes the process of statistical analysis difficult to impossible.

Enter employers again; telling the government that the old way of identifying an applicant would no longer work in today's reality. Then, the agencies responsible for the Uniform Guidelines agreed to redefine "job applicant" so everyone would know what pool of people to base the statistical computations upon. Those agencies were the Equal Employment Opportunity Commission (EEOC), the U.S. Department of Labor, Office of Federal Contract Compliance Programs (OFCCP), the U.S. Department of Justice (DOJ) and the Office of Personnel Management (OPM). They had originally produced and put their signatures to the 1978 regulations, so they were the agencies charged with creating any updates required.

The original charge came several years ago. And, the agencies in their conversations with one another were unable to agree on the definition of job applicant in the new employment environment. So, discussions went on. And, on. And, on. Deadlines were set by the Office of Management and Budget (OMB) for the group to submit its work. Deadlines were extended by OMB again, and again, and again. Until months turned into years, and the task force still had not reached agreement.

After all that, we now have an agreement among the agencies. Rather than change any of the Uniform Guidelines or existing Questions and Answers, the Task Force has elected to add another set of Questions and Answers as a supplement to the original.

The problem for employers has been trying to identify race and sex for job applicants that come through the Internet. Shear volume of submissions has overwhelmed employers. The internet has drastically increased the number of resumes received by organizations and poses additional problems as to who is an applicant.

Questions that employers have been wrestling with include:

- Do unsolicited resumes count as applicants?
- Do we have to invite people who send unsolicited resumes to identify their race and sex?
- Do we have to count people who send resumes, applications or statements of interest if we don't have a job opening?
- Do we have to include people who aren't interviewed?
- Do we have to include people who aren't qualified?

These and many other questions have been answered by employers based on their own procedures as directed in the original Question and Answer #15. The question was: "What is meant by the terms 'applicant' and 'candidate' as they are used in the Uniform Guidelines?" The answer was, "The precise definition of the term 'applicant' depends upon the user's recruitment and selection procedures. The concept of an applicant is that of a person who has indicated an interest in being considered for hiring, promotion, or other employment opportunities. This interest might be expressed by completing an application form, or might be expressed orally, depending upon the employer's practice."

"The term 'candidate' has been included to cover those situations where the initial step by the user involves consideration of current employees for promotion, or training, or other employment opportunities, without inviting applications. The procedure by which persons are identified as candidates is itself a selection procedure under the Guidelines."

The summer of 2004 brought this determination as a result of much input from employers. In order for an individual to be an applicant in the context of the Internet and related electronic data processing technologies, the following must have occurred:

1. The employer has acted to fill a particular position;
2. The individual has followed the employer's standard procedures for submitting applications; and
3. The individual has indicated an interest in the particular position.

To elaborate on the three prongs of this test:

1. The employer has acted to fill a particular position.

   An example under the first prong is:

   Example A: Individuals who register online for Customer Service Representative positions with an Internet and cable television service provider are asked to complete online personal profiles for the employer's resume database. The company acts to fill two vacancies at its Cincinnati Center, and identifies 200 recruits from the database who have indicated that they are available to work in the Cincinnati area. One hundred of these people respond affirmatively and timely to the employer's inquiry about current interest in the particular Cincinnati vacancies. Even if the employer chooses to interview only 25 people for the position, all 100 are UGESP (Uniform Guidelines on Employee Selection Procedures) 'applicants.'

2. The individual has followed the employer's standard procedures for submitting applications.

   If everyone who applies online must complete an online personal profile, only those individuals who do so can be UGESP applicants. If job seekers must use an electronic kiosk or contact a store manager to apply for a sales position, only those who do so can be UGESP applicants. If an employer e-mails online job seekers to ask if they are currently interested in a particular vacancy, only those who meet the employer's deadline can be UGESP applicants. These procedures and directions must be nondiscriminatory because recruitment and the application processes are subject to Title VII and Executive Order 11246.

3. The individual has indicated an interest in the particular position.

   The core of being an 'applicant' is asking to be hired to do a particular job for a specific employer. An individual can only accurately assess her interest in an employment opportunity of which she is aware.

With respect to Internet recruiting, this means that people who post resumes in third party resume banks or on personal Web sites are not UGESP 'applicants' for all employers who search those sites. By posting a resume, the individual is advertising her credentials to the world and indicating a willingness to consider applying for new positions that may be brought to her attention. The individual is not indicating an interest in a particular position with a specific employer. If an employer contacts this individual about a particular position after finding her resume or personal profile online, and the individual indicates an interest in that position, then the individual becomes a UGESP 'applicant,' if she also meets the second prong of the test set forth above. Similarly, if an employer contacts an individual about a particular position in response to an unsolicited resume submitted online, and the individual indicates an interest in that position, then the individual becomes a UGESP 'applicant' if she also meets the second prong test.

Furthermore, even if an individual expresses an interest in a whole category of positions in response to an employer's solicitation—for example, marketing opportunities—the individual is not an applicant but is identifying the kinds of positions in which she may be interested. She is not indicating an interest in a particular position with a specific employer. It is only with respect to a particular position that an individual can assess her interest and choose whether or not to apply."

So, there you have it. We now know what an applicant is when it comes through one of the new technology sources. All employers who are subject to the Uniform Guidelines are obliged to request race and sex identification from job applicants. How an employer does that is left to the employer. The only requirement is that it is a non-discriminatory procedure and the race/sex information is not made available to anyone involved in the selection process.

This makes it more necessary to have a standard procedure for submitting applications for your organization.

Some people define "applicant" as "those people interviewed." While this may be the simplest method, it may only be valid if you actually interviewed every single person applying since if you chose to interview some, but not others, you actually made a selection decision in that process, and that is what is being evaluated. So, this definition may get you in trouble without much line of defense.

There are essentially four things to be considered in determining who your applicants are: 1) was there a decision made, either to go ahead with this person or to stop in the process, "Go/No Go"; 2) was there actually an opportunity available (did the person state an actual job your have available, or did they merely state something like "any" or "anything available" on their application or resume?); 3) using the basic selection devices to be used in the process (to be discussed in more detail later); and, 4) were your procedures uniformly applied? It is for this reason that I would recommend you do not accept any unsolicited applications/resumes and you rule out any applications/resume that do not specify a job/position for which you are seeking applicants. Remember, it's important that you COUNT THE RIGHT NUMBERS in your analyses. This means you count all of those you made some type of Go—No Go decision on for each of your opportunities. Not many companies have position title of "Any" or "Anything available."

Some might be asking what is this "Go—No Go" you have mentioned? This is simply if you have made a decision based on a comparison of their knowledge, skills, and abilities with those which are required of the job, you have made a "Go—No Go" decision on that individual, who has now become an "applicant." With this in mind if you do not receive unsolicited application/resumes, you should either send them back to the sender or simply throw them out. If you decide to keep them you should mark them as "Unsolicited/Not Considered", or other such designation. This would also apply to those resumes you receive over the Internet. The important thing to keep in mind here is that you must treat all such unsolicited applications/resumes the same. If you "cherry pick" just one of those you must consider all received as "applicants."

There are several other things you might consider in determining who your applicants are or are not. You might refuse to consider those applications/resume that you receive after the deadline you have established (presuming you did), or if there was no specific job listed as what they were applying for (as mentioned above), or you may have other criteria such as they misspelled the Company's name, or other idiosyncrasies. The important thing is to be consistent.

Another thing you should do is to remove any person who by their own actions takes themselves out of the process. These would be people you attempt to call to arrange an interview, but are unable to reach them. It would also include those people who do not show up for their interview, or turn down an opportunity for an interview. These are people that you did not make an employment decision on, but in fact, took themselves out of the running. Do not count them in your analyses. You did not reject them, they eliminated themselves. COUNT THE RIGHT NUMBERS.

By all means do not forget those individuals to whom you made an offer of employment to, but for some reason did not begin employment. These might be those individuals who reject your offer due to any number of reasons or they may be those individuals you made any offer to contingent upon the successful completion of, say, a negative drug screen, but they turned up positive, and there are also those who actually accept your offer, but simply don't show up for work. These people were a positive selection decision and should be recorded as such. If you don't record them as a positive they will reflect as a negative in your calculations. COUNT THE RIGHT NUMBERS.

Earlier we mentioned the basic selection devices used by the Company in making their decision. These could be the process you will follow in order to ascertain who will be hired for your opportunity. This process might include how you are going to evaluate the applications/resumes, what are you looking for that these documents will provide? Are you going to administer any pre-employment tests? If so what type? Are they content valid? Hopefully, they are not either psychological or intelligence tests as they are too subjective and allow for more problems for the contractor than whatever good might come. You might consider any interview criteria, such as eye contact, presentation skills, appearance, verification of data given on the application/resume, or other such criteria. It might even come down to liking or not liking, the "gut feeling", all other things considered.

Other things you might consider in your selection process are references, drug screens, physical exams, and/or criminal records. The important thing is to be consistent throughout your process with all of your applicants.

One other thing to mention in the hiring process is that you might well have an opportunity in which you have a mixed pool of applicants. That is you have external as well as internal (existing employees) applicants. If such is the case you must consider the employees as a part of the applicant "pool" and use them in your calculations in determining either disparate treatment or disparate impact.

The important thing to remember is that you have a definition of what makes an applicant, and you follow your definition in all cases.

The OFCCP recommends the contractor should apply the "4/5ths or 80 percent rule" to determine whether the selection rates are sufficiently substantial to be regarded as evidence of adverse impact. Under this rule if a selection for a particular group (gender, or race) is less than 4/5ths or 80 percent of the selection rate for the group with the highest selection rate it is generally regarded as evidence of adverse impact. In way of showing this we use the following scenario:

Job Title: Engineer
Total Male applicants:     40
Males hired/offered:       20
% Males hired/offered:     50.0%

Total Female applicants:         100
Females hired/offered:            20
% Females hired/offered:       20.0%

The highest selection rate is the 50% for White Males so this is the figure used to base your calculations on.
50% x 80% (4/5ths) = 40%
White Females = 20.0%, which is less than 40%, therefore adverse impact is indicated.

What we have just done is to calculate the "Selection Rate" for those individuals applying for a position as Engineer in our Company and this is the calculation you should make. A common mistake that is made is to calculate the "Hire Rate", which in this case would look as follows:

Job Title: Engineer
Total Hired/Offered:             40

Total Males Hired/Offered:       20
% Males Hired/Offered:         50.0%

Females Hired/Offered:           20
% Females Hired/Offered:       50.0%

As this example shows, you have hired 50% Males and 50% Females. If you mistakenly use the "Hire Rate" you will not know you have a presumption of adverse impact until it is too late. Do not use "Hire Rate" as it is wrong and dangerous because it may lead to bad decisions and a false sense of security.

The 80 percent rule is not the required calculation to be used in calculating adverse impact. It is simply one mentioned by the OFCCP as a method to be used. They like it because of its simplicity. They also recognize that sample size and other factors can affect the reliability of this calculation as a measure of adverse impact.

# Our Selection Process

## Promotions

In order to best analyze your selection decisions in promotional situations, you need to first know what constitutes a promotion. Promotions are those opportunities within an organization where an individual advances to a position where one or more of the following is present: an increase in pay, an increase in responsibility and/or authority, or a need for a higher level of skills. For example, a person is promoted from an Engineering Drafter to that of Industrial Engineer would be a promotion, as it would more than likely involve a raise in salary, a higher degree of responsibility, and a need for a higher level of skill. However, giving an Engineering Drafter a pay raise would not constitute a promotion as everything else would remain the same and they raise in pay may only be as a result of performance.

Promotions usually involve having to make a selection decision from a list of candidates, or internal applicants. When you have an opportunity, internal or external, it is important that you begin a "Job Packet" for that opportunity. In this packet you will have a copy of each of the applications. In the case of these internal applicants you will know the gender and race/ethnicity and you will know their existing job. Keep track of what you did with each of the applicants throughout the process of deciding who would get the promotion. This "pool" will form the basis for making your selection rate for promotion calculations.

One must also look at those promotions that are such that an individual would simply move from, say Accountant I to Accountant II. Such a promotion may be based on performance, seniority, or some other criteria, but often times does not involve considering others in the promotion. This type would be a "non-competitive" promotion where no other people are considered. It is strongly recommended that at least annually, when you update your AAP, you list those employees who are candidates for advancement during the upcoming year. This list will also be helpful in determining training programs and further career development measures taken for those employees you identify as having potential beyond their present positions.

At the time you perform your calculations it is, once again, important to COUNT THE RIGHT NUMBERS.

In analyzing your promotions you will simply take each of your Job Packets and take the number of Males applying for the opportunity and how many Males were selected, and the number of Females applying and how many Females were selected. The resulting percentages would be the selection rate percentage for promotion in this particular opportunity. For example, 10 Males bid on the opportunity and 4 were selected or 40%. 10 Females bid on the same opportunity and 2 was selected or 20%. Using the 80% Rule it would be discovered there is a presumption of discrimination toward Females applying for this opportunity (40% x 80% = 32%, which is higher than the 20% of Females selected.)

Some perform a percentage of persons promoted calculation as follows: 6 people were promoted, and 2 were Females. The promotion rate was 33.3%. This calculation is incorrect and should not be used in your analyses.

A brief note on the importance of the "Job Packet." If you do not have a listing of those actually considered for each of your promotion opportunities the OFCCP will determine your candidates to be the entire Job Group from which the successful employee came out of. This might not only skew your data so it doesn't really give you much information as to what took place in your selection process, which will make it difficult to correct if need be, but it might create a presumption of discrimination that in actuality does not exist. Again, it cannot be stressed enough: COUNT THE RIGHT NUMBERS!

Another important detail that might be included in the Job Packet might be the selection criteria used in the selection process. Such criteria might include things as performance appraisals, attendance, time on the job, recommendations from supervisors, or other "qualifications." These might be useful if you have to defend any part of the process.

# NOTES

# Terminations

Hires and Promotions are sometimes referred to as "Positive Selections" because they deal with positive outcomes. Terminations on the other hand are "Negative Selections" as they deal with such actions as resignations, retirement, disability, or other type of termination of employment. Such terminations are referred to as "Voluntary" as they are the choice of the incumbent.

Other types of termination are "Involuntary" as they are the result of contractor choice. Examples of involuntary terminations are discharge for cause, reductions in force (RIF), persons who might be continued on payroll during pay-out of severance.

The two types of termination are mentioned as each should be analyzed separately. You simply would compute the selection rate by dividing those selected for termination by those who were considered for termination for each of the groups, males vs. females, whites vs. minorities.

While it is true those terminations identified as "Voluntary" do not have a "pool" and are not a decision made by the employer, they are considered as important from a risk management standpoint as they may present a "red flag" as to something occurring within the organization that may be "forcing" certain groups to leave. Such occurrences could be discriminatory and could bring major "issues" in the future if not rectified. For example, are women leaving in disproportionate numbers from the accounting department? Is there the possibility of harassment? Do they feel they are at a dead end with no chance for advancement? Are there other circumstances causing this?

The same might be true for "Involuntary" terminations.

In the case of computing reductions in force terminations you should have your reduction "plan" established prior to the termination. This plan would include the criteria used to determine who would be terminated. Such criteria might include performance appraisals, seniority, job abolishment, ability to perform remaining work, and other criteria appropriate to your situation. The important thing would be having the criteria and using it in your selection process.

# NOTES

# RESPONSIBILITIES FOR IMPLEMENTATION

## §60-2.17(a)

The requirements of your Affirmative Action Plan includes documentation of who is responsible for the overall program as well as what they are responsible for. The OFCCP states that the person responsible should be an official of the company of an authoritative level. This individual should be designated as the director or manager of the company's Affirmative Action activities and whose identity should appear on all internal and external communications regarding the company's Affirmative Action programs. This individual must be given necessary top management support and staff to manage the implementation of the program.

In larger organizations this might actually be a "chain of command" from the top executive, having "ultimate" responsibility, to another individual, such as the Director of Human Resources, who in turn might oversee the actual carrying out of the program by maybe a Human Resource Manager. Whatever your situation, it is important that the reporting relationship be clearly established to run directly to the President/CEO of your organization, at least for affirmative action purposes.

This section of the narrative of your plan will include all of those areas of responsibility. Some actually use this section as simply restating the job description of the Affirmative Action Officer of the company. In some larger organizations affirmative action may be the only function of this individual; however, in most this person will have other responsibilities. In either event this person must have the necessary support of top management in order to comply with the regulations and this must be clearly stated in the narrative of your plan document.

The regulations indicate the following activities as satisfying the responsibility regulations and this could actually be a job description for the individual designated as the official in charge of the Affirmative Action Program:

1.   Develop policy statements, Affirmative Action programs and internal and external communication techniques. The OFCCP states that supervisors should be advised that:

   a.   Their work performance is being evaluated on the basis of their Affirmative Action efforts and results, as well as other criteria.
      1.   This should be stressed because without the commitment of managers and supervisors the Affirmative Action program cannot succeed. In fact, it can fail miserably without that commitment. It is the opinion that including behaviors toward Affirmative Action on performance reviews goes a long way toward gaining this commitment.

   b.   The company is obligated to prevent harassment of employees placed through Affirmative Action efforts.

2.   Identification of problem areas. The Affirmative Action officer is expected to assist in such activities as reviewing regular data reports like computer printouts of company progress in the employment of minorities and females. These reports would summarize the contractor's actual staff contrasted with its affirmative action goals and look at reasons for non-goal compliance, such as terminations and other turnover. It is important, however, that in this section the actual names of those reports not be made since that might only give the OFCCP something else to request.

3.      Designing and implementing audit and reporting systems that:
   a.   Measure the effectiveness of the company's programs.
   b.   Indicate the need for remedial action.
   c.   Determine the degree to which the company's objectives have been attained.
   d.   Determine whether known disabled veterans and other eligible veterans have had the opportunity to participate in all company spon-

sored educational training, recreational and social activities. This
would also apply to minorities and women.

    e.    Ensure that each location is in compliance with the Act and the regulations in this part.

4.    Serve as liaison between the company and enforcement agencies.

5.    Serve as liaison between the company and organization of and for disabled veterans and veterans of the Vietnam era, and arrange for the active involvement by company representatives in the community service programs of local organizations of and for disabled veterans and other eligible veterans.

6.    Keep management informed of the latest development in the entire Affirmative Action area.

7.    Assist line management in arriving at solutions to problems is a responsibility of the Affirmative Action Officer. It is important to emphasize the officer's efforts. If the officer meets with managers and supervisors to discuss goal attainment and plan progress, and works with them in formulating affirmative action initiatives, these activities should be referenced in this section of the plan.

Most put the responsibility of providing career counseling on the Affirmative Action Officer. However, it is my opinion this is better provided by line management personnel as who knows the specific job functions and what development is necessary than those individuals? The Affirmative Action Officer should see that such counseling is taking place, but not be doing the actual counseling, at least not in all areas of the organization.

It is extremely important to include concrete examples of initiatives undertaken by the affirmative action officer, rather than merely paraphrasing the regulations. In other words make it a document of what you are doing rather than what the regulations say you should be doing.

# NOTES

# IDENTIFICATION OF PROBLEM AREAS

## §60-2.17(b)

This section is the most sensitive and by far the most comprehensive of the required areas to be reported in your documentation and will take the most skill and care in writing. This section is the report of your findings resulting from the analyses you make on your progress during the prior year. It is intended, by the regulations, to be a critical self-analysis where the contractor shows in detail organizational unit and determines whether there is any evidence of adverse impact against minorities and/or women, and also reports on virtually all other phases of your compliance, including technical compliance with the affirmative action requirements. While every contractor acting in good faith in being critical in its self-analysis, you must be extremely careful in how the findings are reported as confidentiality is not guaranteed and disclosure under the Freedom of Information Act (FOIA) can make this section extremely valuable to a plaintiff's attorney.

The principal concern is that anything critical said in this section potentially can be used against you in administrative or court litigation. While you are obliged to make a full analysis as set forth in the regulations, you can, and should, take extreme caution in the language you use to report the findings. You should write the results in as positive fashion as possible, staying away from an actual admission of discrimination or ineffective affirmative action.

Whenever you identify anything as being a problem area you should also take great care to provide whatever objective explanation exists for the apparent problem. For example, one of the more prevalent problem areas is that of a problem being discovered in a particular job group during your analysis of selection decisions. Your report should not end with merely stating you came up short, but you might evaluate the applicant flow data and discover, for example, that you actually made job offers to a number of minorities and/or women who for some reason were not employed. They may have turned down your offer or they may not have showed up for work, for some reason. In any event their not being actually employed was not a matter of your not selecting them, they rejected you and this should not be held against you, therefore you might report such occurrences. Or the problem discovered may have been the result of insufficient numbers of minorities or women applying for those jobs. You might explain what efforts you undertook to attract higher numbers of minorities and women in order to correct the situation. The point here is, do not merely stop at reporting you had a problem without also stating what you are doing to solve that problem.

At the same time it is important when reporting an instance where you identify something as a potential problem that you supply non-discriminatory, objective reasons for why the situation exists.

Now that the significance of this section has been established let's look at those areas you should be evaluating and reporting on in this section.

The first area to be analyzed is the <u>composition of the workforce by minority group status and sex.</u> This is typically accomplished through the **Workforce Analysis** or **Organizational Profile**, and the **Utilization Analysis**. Each of these analyses will be discussed more fully in another chapter of this book. For purposes here know these analyses will be reported in this section of your narrative document.

At this point in the "written" documentation I do not recommend going into a long discussion of the calculations and do not recommend listing the statistics. Instead I direct the reader to the Exhibits section of the documentation where they may find the actual analyses. A discussion of the results by Job Group and by Organizational Unit will follow later in this section under the appropriate heading.

The <u>compositions of applicant flow data by minority group status and sex</u> will also be evaluated and reported in this section. This is where you should explain your method of keeping applicant flow data, any problems that this method may have had, and what you are doing to correct those problems. For example, you might indicate you were unable to retrieve or match up data with specific decisions.

In order to correct this you may now be using "Job Packets" for each opportunity you have in order to keep track of each applicant for each decision you made in the hiring process.

If your EEO Self-Identification Form was a problem you might indicate such and what you are planning to do to correct it. If it was adequate you might want to state that. Remember, bring out positive you are doing as well as those areas identified as problems.

The total selection process including position descriptions, position titles, position specifications, application forms, job posting procedures, referral procedures, final selection process, and similar factors. All of these areas should be evaluated and responded to. Again, the positive as well as the problem areas (with explanation of those problem areas.)

An example might be: "All position descriptions have been reviewed, with changes made, where necessary, to accurately reflect current job duties. Jobs have been classified, especially for compensation purposes, to similarly classify those requiring substantially similar skill, effort, and responsibility. Position descriptions establish job-related and non-discriminatory requirements."

You might do the same for your evaluation of job titles, making sure none of them give preference to one gender or another.

Next, an evaluation of your transfer and promotion practices would be in order, followed by a discussion of the findings. If your selections are made on the basis of knowledge, skills, and abilities and without regard to race, color, sex, religion, or national origin, you might be well advised to mention such in your narrative. You might also want to evaluate whether all employees are encouraged to take advantage of the opportunities and to apply when such come about. If you do this, tell it in your narrative. I cannot mention often enough to take advantage of what you are doing well. Put it in your narrative.

Evaluate your facilities, company-sponsored recreation and social events to make sure none are segregated in any way and that recreation and social events are open to all employees. Report your findings in your narrative.

What type of company training and apprenticeship programs do you make available to your employees? Are these available to all employees, without regard to race, color, sex, religion, or national origin? If you have no apprenticeship programs you might indicate such in your narrative.

Does your company have a seniority system? <u>Is there evidence that seniority practices contribute to disparity based on race or sex?</u> If there is no seniority system in your organization state that in the narrative.

What is the <u>attitude of workforce managers and supervisors?</u> Hopefully, you are able to report a positive attitude towards the company's EEO and Affirmative Action policies by the managers and supervisors.

Next, you should mention those <u>technical phases of compliance, such as posters, retention of applications, etc.</u> For example, "Current posters have been placed on employee bulletin boards." "ABC Company retains solicited applications and resumes for a period of two years from the date they are received, or from the date a selection is made, whichever is later." (This need only be 1 year if your organization has fewer than 150 employees.)

The above mentioned areas are those relating primarily to your organization's policies and practices. The next area is the identification of problem areas by Job Group.

It is here that you would mention that a Utilization Analysis has been conducted in an effort to determine whether you had any Job Groups in which there were fewer minorities and/or women than would reasonably be expected based on their availability. You might also use this section to explain the methodology you employed in this analysis and identify those Job Groups in which underutilization exists and establishing responsive goals for those Job Groups. You might also restate, assuming you already did in the Preface of your document, that "underutilization" is used only because it is used in the regulations, and its usage does not constitute any admission of wrong doing on your part.

The next area to be discussed is the <u>identification of problem areas by Organizational Unit.</u> In their effort to determine whether there is any under representation or concentration among your organizational units the OFCCP uses the Job Area Acceptance Range (JAAR). The regulations contain no mention of "problem areas" or "deficiencies" by organizational unit. The establishment of "goals and objectives" if and when a contractor has identified "problem areas" in any organizational unit is required, however there is no regulatory definition on what constitutes a "problem area"; there also is no description in the published regulations regarding the nature of any required goals. It is our understanding that such goals and objectives are not numerical (in contrast to goals in under-utilized Job Groups) but rather are action-oriented efforts such as improved recruitment efforts.

As mentioned above, some compliance officers use the so-called JAAR method to evaluate <u>distribution</u>—as distinguished from <u>utilization</u>, which is a function of the availability of minorities and women with requisite skills, irre-spective of departmental participation. To the best of our knowledge, the JAAR approach has neither statutory nor regulatory foundation.

By definition, the JAAR method assumes that it is problematic if minorities and women are not evenly distributed throughout the contractor's various work units. This assumption exists irrespective of the size of the department. More importantly, it exists irrespective of the diverse skills required by the positions in various departments and the varying availabilities—applicant flow—of minori-ties and women possessing those skills.

To determine the "acceptance range" requires an "averaging" of the workforce. Where there is an aggregation of incumbents throughout the work force, or even within certain components (exempt versus non-exempt, for example), the result-ing "acceptance range" is fundamentally flawed. In truth, "under representa-tions"—participation lower than the "acceptance range" (which is not to be confused with "underutilization")—are likely to be the result of a lack of minor-ity and/or female applicants. Further, attempts to correct "concentration" (a par-ticipation rate higher than the "acceptance range") may themselves lead to adverse impact in selections. Perhaps these serious conceptual flaws explain why there has never been any regulation adopting this method of examining the workforce.

In any event, it is our opinion that only a properly executed discrimination analysis can reveal whether there are any "problems" by organizational unit or department. Therefore, we do not use the JAAR in our examination of organiza-tional unit.

It is recommended you examine your selection decisions by Job Group (pursuant to the wishes of the OFCCP) and by job title (pursuant to the regulations) where there were sufficient selections to make such an analysis possible.

It is also recommended that if you decide to not use the JAAR in making your examination you explain, similar to the explanation given above, in your narrative why you did not use it.

In conclusion, make this self-analysis at least annually and examine your program most rigorously, but watch what you record and how you record it. You need not record the results of that analysis in every detail. This section is to be a genuine self-audit, so include "confessions of failure" where they do not involve discrimination or where they are going to be obvious (such as keeping applicant flow logs or having application forms that ask about arrest records or name of relative for "emergency" contact), but do s in the most self-serving way possible.

Use your confidential communication systems (including through counsel, if necessary) to convey blunt hard facts about potential liability and discrimination systems. The AAP has a much wider readership and is, generally, discoverable. Woe to the AAP writer who provides ammunition to the Plaintiff.

# NOTES

# DEVELOPMENT AND IMPLEMENTATION OF ACTION-ORIENTED PROGRAMS

## §60-2.17(c)

This section of your Affirmative Action Plan is intended to relate closely to the Identification of Problem Areas section of your Plan. In the Problems Area section you identified those areas where your self-audit identified those areas where additional affirmative action is required. Once you have identified a problem you then develop a specific action-oriented program designed to remedy that problem.

In developing an action-oriented program remember it is more simply put, a goal. This makes it easier to include all of the aspects the OFCCP would be looking for should they audit your program. You should include the "who", "what", "how", and "when" in your documentation of the action-oriented program. What is the action to be taken? Who will accomplish it? How will it be accomplished? When will it be accomplished? By writing it in this manner you will be able to better track the progress made, making adjustments where necessary.

The revised regulations place a greater interest in this section than was previously taken by the OFCCP. The agency is examining closely whether the contractor has sufficiently developed and implemented specific action-oriented programs, which are designed to address those actual problem areas identified in the course of your self-analysis. For example, if it was discovered you are actually not getting sufficient minority or women applicants for specific job groups in your recruitment efforts, what action(s) are you going to take to increase minority or women applicants in those specific job groups when you have opportunities in the future? The agency generally recognizes that it is the contractor's

86

responsibility to develop and execute action-oriented programs. However, it takes the position that its responsibility is to evaluate two primary areas; 1) whether or not the action-oriented programs you have developed are specific enough and result oriented enough to accomplish the aim for which they were created, and 2) whether or not the action-oriented programs were properly executed.

The OFCCP will look to see if the activities you have included in your program are tailored to EEO-1 categories or job groups where you have indicated an underutilization as they preferably should be.

The regulations suggest that you conduct the following in this section:

1.  The contractor should conduct a detailed analysis of job descriptions to insure that they accurately describe the duties and responsibilities of the position, and are consistent for the same position from one location or branch to another. Further, your descriptions should be reviewed to make sure they do not include factors which involve bias with respect to race, color, ethnicity, sex, religion, or national origin.

2.  You should validate worker specifications by division, department, location or other organizational unit and also by the job title using job performance criteria. In this process you should look at experience, education and skill requirements to ensure that the requirements in themselves do not constitute discrimination. Should a job be found to screen out a disproportionate number of minorities or women it should be professionally validated to job performance. The OFCCP in your area will provide you with names of companies that conduct validation studies. You should also indicate that special attention has been given to academic experience and skill requirements to insure that these requirements do not in themselves constitute inadvertent discrimination.

3.  Job descriptions and specifications, when used by your company, should be made available to all of the management employees involved in the recruiting, screening, selection, and promotion process. The job descriptions should also be sent to your recruiting sources.

88 • Develop an Affirmative Action Program as a Risk Management Tool

4.  You should evaluate your entire selection process to ensure that the process does not contain areas of hidden bias.

5.  It is important that the individuals conducting the recruiting, screening, selection, promotions, disciplinary, and related procedures be carefully selected and trained to ensure elimination of bias in all personnel actions.

6.  Your company must observe the requirements of the OFCCP Order pertaining to test validation and other selection procedures. This is one area you can run into potential problems without realizing it. Invariably a manager or supervisor will feel they need to implement some sort of "screening" device and it, in fact, may be doing just that—screening out minorities or women. Make certain any devices you use in your selection procedures are content valid. That is pertinent to the job, such as a typing test for a job in which typing skills are mandatory or welding skills in the case of a welding job. If you are in doubt as to the validity of a test or other procedure you should contact a professional in the area of validation or you might contact the local office of the OFCCP for assistance.

7.  Some types of selection practices other than tests may also be used which might have the effect of discriminating against women or minorities. The OFCCP lists some of these practices as unscored interviews, unscored or casual application forms, arrest records, credit checks, considerations of marital status or dependency of minor children. Where your company may have a record of these types of unfair discrimination or exclusion of minorities or women the company should eliminate them if they are not objectively valid.

8.  It is quite typical for a contractor to have to increase the flow of minority and female applicants and this may vary from job group to job group. The regulations suggest you contact organizations within your recruitment area in addition to the State Employment Service. You contact organizations such as the Job Corp, Neighborhood Youth Corps, Secondary Schools, Colleges and university programs (particularly predominantly minority and/or women schools). The National Organization for Women, Welfare Rights Organizations, Business and Professional Women's organizations, American Association of University

Women, YWCA, and the National Council of Negro Women are a few examples of groups you may consider working with in order to increase minority and female applicants to your job opportunities.

9.  You might invite representatives from the organizations you identify to work with to tour your facility and review job descriptions so they can provide accurate information to prospective job applicants. You might also explain your selection process and distribute any recruiting information or company information you have available. You might also agree on formal recruiting procedures that will be used between your company and the organization so the recruitment will proceed in a manner beneficial to both your company and the applicant.

10. A special effort should be made to recruit women and minorities for positions in the human resource department.

11. Your company should participate in Career Days, Minority Youth Employment Programs, Job Fairs, and in special recruiting programs for minorities and women at colleges, high schools, and universities. Not only might this be beneficial to your affirmative action efforts it makes sound business sense, particularly in a tight labor market.

12. You should also have a program for internal promotions that will provide for the advancement of minorities and women. Such a program might include the following:
    a.  You might have a formal career counseling program in place.
    b.  Vacancy announcements are posted at the facility in a conspicuous place for all to view.
    c.  You should have an inventory of current minority and female employees, including review of education, skills, and experience.
    d.  Remedial training and work-study programs have been developed.
    e.  Formal employee evaluation programs and processes have been implemented.
    f.  Worker specifications have been validated based on job performance criteria.

g.  Justification is required when apparently qualified minority or female employees are passed over for promotion, particularly in goal areas.

h.  Seniority practices should be reviewed for adverse impact.

We have discussed several aspects of your program that would be addressed in this section of your AAP and they all have the common thread of involving a selection decision by members of your management team. These particular areas involve the company's policies and practices, recruitment, and promotions. There are, of course, other areas in which employment decisions are made that were not mentioned above and these might be examined as well. For example, if you had a reduction in force (RIF) you might discuss the procedures followed in determining who was terminated. This might fall under the policies and practices. You may have had a disproportionate number of minorities or women resign or quit from a given job group. As this may be a "red flag" for a compliance officer you might discuss it and what remediation you plan to take in the future.

Remember, this is a very key section of the AAP. The suggestions for implementation mentioned above provide you with good foundations but there is certainly flexibility in choosing what methods you intend to employ. The main thing is that you act affirmatively and be prepared to demonstrate how you have done so. It is not sufficient to conduct "business as usual" when you have identified specific problems. This section is the proof of your good faith efforts.

# NOTES

# Internal Audits and Reporting Systems

## §60-2.17(d)

The fourth section to be in your narrative in accordance with the regulations is a discussion of your internal audits and reporting systems. The best Affirmative Action Plan cannot be successful if you develop it and forget about it until it's time to write the program for the following year. You must audit the program and develop a reporting system to determine whether or not the Affirmative Action Plan is working. In the first three sections of your plan you have assigned responsibilities for each facet of your program, you have identified problem areas and developed programs to resolve those problem areas. Now you develop the mechanisms you will use to monitor your program throughout the life of the Plan. In order to accomplish this, the following guidelines have been set up by the OFCCP:

1. The person responsible for the Affirmative Action Plan should set up a system to monitor the records of referrals, placements, transfers, promotions, and terminations. This should be done for all activities at all levels of your company to ensure that the company's policy of nondiscrimination is actually being carried out. Your narrative should explain how you monitor those activities. You should explain how this data is collected and how they are analyzed. Basically, you should indicate your familiarity with the types of data and analyses necessary to determine progress within your Affirmative Action Program.

2. Your Affirmative Action Program will be more successful if supervisors and managers are held accountable for their actions in regard to EEO and Affirmative Action. In this regard the OFCCP requires that formal

reports be required from managers to explain their progress in meeting Affirmative Action Program goals with respect to unit goal attainment. The agency feels that it is only through goals being broken down to component levels that the contractor can hope to meet its overall facility goals. Steps taken by the contractor such as training, evaluation of supervisory performance based in part on goal attainment, and provision of regular progress reports to line management should be described.

3.   The individual responsible for the Affirmative Action Program should review the results of the Affirmative Action Plan with all levels of management. It is often beneficial to hold meetings to review the progress and answer questions regarding Affirmative Action/EEO. In addition, you may want to review any recent court cases or regulations which may affect your company.

4.   The individual responsible for the Affirmative Action Program should advise top management of the program effectiveness and submit recommendations to improve unsatisfactory performance. This could be done on a quarterly basis in way of a review of goal accomplishment for each department and job group so that management can see where goals are being accomplished and good faith efforts are being made. It is a good idea to conduct regular meetings with top management to advise them of Affirmative Action progress and update them on any recent court decisions that might affect your company. This keeps the topic of affirmative action in the forefront.

Sophisticated contractors have developed internal auditing systems based on their knowledge of the organization. They have tracked particular supervisors, departments, divisions whose success at and perhaps commitment to affirmative action has been questionable. The OFCCP regularly requests access to such information as part of its compliance reviews. Therefore, you would be well advised to develop, and report such systems in your narrative.

# NOTES

# COMPENSATION ANALYSIS

Compensation studies can be categorized as formal and informal. Formal studies, such as equal pay and pay progression studies are preferable for two reasons: 1) they can detect legally recognized forms of employment discrimination, and 2) they employ statistical measures of pay disparities that are a standard part of employment discrimination case law. Informal studies, such as DuBray analysis, offer simple, practical methods for comparing employee salaries along racial or gender lines, but they can be sharply criticized on both legal and statistical grounds. The DuBray is the method generally performed by the OFCCP.

Formal compensation studies fall generally into one of two types: equal pay or pay progression. To detect equal pay, you analyze differences in current pay of employees who are doing the same job or substantially similar jobs. Such groups are called cohorts and they should comprise employees similarly situated with regard to such characteristics as departmental affiliation, pay grade, job title, and seniority. Then you check for differences in current pay within these cohorts along gender and racial lines.

Pay progression analysis is done in order to check for disparate treatment and/or disparate impact discrimination. Disparate treatment occurs when an employer intentionally treats females differently from similarly situated males or members of one racial group differently from similarly situated member of another racial group. Disparate impact discrimination occurs when 1) a policy of the employer applied uniformly to all people who were similarly situated as of some date in the past has the effect of placing disproportionately many people of some race or gender at a disadvantage and 2) that policy does not have an adequate business justification.

# NOTES

# EEO—1 REPORTS

Make sure you have inserted your last three (3) EEO—1 Reports in the Exhibits of your AAP. If you have yet to file the EEO—1 Report you will have to do so. You should contact the Joint Reporting Committee at (757) 461—1213 and inform them that you must file the EEO—1 Report for the first time. This report is due annually on September 30th.

Following is a brief summary of the new EEO-1 Reporting. At present this proposal is still under "comments", but is expected to go into effect in 2005.

Here are the key changes proposed by the EEOC:

1.) In accord with changes made in 1997 to the Standards for the Classification of Federal Data on Race and Ethnicity, "Hispanic or Latino" will be separated from "race" categories and sex data will be reported separately for Hispanic ethnicity. All "Non-Hispanic or Latino" individuals will be reported in one of six race categories by sex.

2.) The race categories will be:

- White
- Black or African American
- Asian
- Native Hawaiian or Other Pacific Islander
- American Indian or Alaska Native

- Two or more races (Any employee indicating a heritage of two or more races will be reported in this column. The specific combinations of multiple races will not be reported.

3.) The Officials and Managers job category on the current form will be expanded into three categories and renamed. They will be called Executive/Senior Level Officials and Managers, Mid-Level Officials and Managers, and Lower-Level Officials and Managers.

4.) Professionals, Technicians and Sales Workers will remain the same. Office and Clerical will change to Administrative Support Workers.

5.) Service Workers will move from category #9 to category #6 and Craft Workers, Operatives, and Laborers and Helpers will move down accordingly.

6.) Totals will be required for both rows and columns.

7.) Totals will also be required for columns showing the previous year employee counts.

To learn more, and to see a PDF version of the actual proposed report format, go to http://www.eeoc.gov/eeo1. You can also obtain a copy of the Federal Register notice at the same web site.

# NOTES

# EQUAL OPPORTUNITY (EO) SURVEY

## §60-2.18

The Equal Opportunity Survey is probably the most notable addition to the revisions that went into effect on December 13, 2000. This document must be taken seriously by contractors as it is going to be the primary "trigger" for initiating Compliance Reviews.

The OFCCP will designate each year a significant number of non-construction contractor establishments to prepare and file an Equal Opportunity Survey (EO Survey). For a copy of this survey contact us at http://h-r-m-s.com/contact. The contractors selected will be notified by the OFCCP. The intent of the Survey is to provide compliance data to the OFCCP early in the compliance evaluation process which will allow the agency to more effectively identify that establishment in need of further evaluation. It is estimated that nearly ½ of the contractors will receive notification to complete the Survey each year. Although the OFCCP indicates that the contractor would expect to be surveyed every other year, there is no defined manner in which a contractor is selected; therefore, it is conceivable a contractor could be selected on an annual basis.

There is a specific format in which the EO Survey is to be completed. As the sample given shows, there are three main parts. Part A is for general information about the contractor. In this part you would be required to supply such information as your establishment's Tax Number, the Federal Contracting Agency and Contract Number, the Date your current AAP expires (this would be for your AAP for women and minorities, your AAP for individuals with disabilities, and your AAP for Veterans), an indication as to whether you had listed any employment openings with your local State Employment Service, and your establishment's address.

Part B requests information pertaining to your employment selection decisions in the areas of applicants, hiring, promotions, and terminations. In responding to this part you will supply by EEO Job Category the activity in each of those areas by sex and race/ethnicity along with the total number of full-time employees at the end of the calendar/AAP year, by sex and race/ethnicity.

Part C is devoted to compensation information, again by EEO Job Category. There are two comparisons made in this section—Minority Female and Non-Minority Female, and Minority Male and Non-Minority Male. The compensation is reported in thousands of dollars, rounded to the nearest thousand in the following groupings:

Total Annual Monetary Compensation for All Minority Female Employees
Lowest Annual Monetary Compensation of any Single Minority Female Employee
Highest Annual Monetary Compensation for any Single Minority Female Employee
Average Tenure of Minority Female Employee (Years and Months)

The same information is then prepared for Non-Minority Female Employees. In the second section of Part C you would supply the same information for Minority Male employees and Non-Minority Male employees.

It is the OFCCP's believe this information will allow for an accurate assessment of contractor personnel activities, pay practices, and affirmative action performance. As use of the EO Survey develops the Department may at some time determine that one or more of the data elements currently included should be altered or deleted and they have made provisions for this in the regulations. In the event they deem it necessary to make a change in the format, the following must exists:

The Secretary must clearly demonstrate through statistical analyses of EO Survey submissions that the data element in question is no longer of value; and the Secretary must follow Notice and Comment procedures.

If you are notified you have to prepare a Survey you will be encouraged to submit it via the Internet. However, you could also send it via fax to the telephone number indicated in the Survey instructions. Paper versions of the EO Survey must be mailed to the address indicated in the Survey instructions. The filing deadline will be specified by the Deputy Assistant Secretary.

The regulations state the OFCCP will treat this information as confidential to the maximum extent the information is exempt from public disclosure under the Freedom of Information Act, 5 U.S.C. 552. It would be a good idea to have a confidentiality statement accompany your completed Survey indicating the sensitivity of the information to your business and the release of the data would subject your establishment to commercial harm.

# NOTES

# PROGRAM SUMMARY

## §60-2.31

Your Affirmative Action Program must be summarized and updated annually. The Program Summary must be prepared in a format which will be prescribed by the Deputy Assistant Secretary and published in the Federal Register as a notice before becoming effective. Contractors and subcontractors must submit the Program Summary to OFCCP each year on the anniversary date of the Affirmative Action Program.

You may get more information regarding the Program Summary at http://h-r-m-s.com/contact.

# Other Risk Management Considerations

## Employee Morale

An area often neglected when evaluating things such as safety, quality, productivity and even things such as litigations is the mental climate of the employees. Up until now this book has dealt itself with those areas of affirmative action which are required through the regulations. You have evaluated those areas in which your organization has made employment decisions and have given more detailed considerations to those areas where you may have come up short. You have looked at what you have done, evaluated the results, and formulated plans of attack on correcting those things needing adjustment.

You have looked at what you have done with the outcomes, but another consideration might be looking at what the employees can tell you about how the organization flows from their perspective. Experience shows that people who feel they are listened to tend to feel they make a difference in the success or failure of whatever they are doing and, therefore, are typically more involved, or committed to the success of that group or organization.

A committed employee is more likely to be considered as a "good employee" because they are better producers and tend to be less apt to have a history of on the job accidents, less absenteeism, and have fewer complaints that may lead to costly litigations.

One method that has proven successful in letting the employees have input is to conduct an employee opinion survey every 18-24 months. These are best conducted by an outside third party as the employees are more receptive to voicing their opinions when anonymity is ensured. To the employer the important thing is to learn how the employee base perceives the organization.

## Assessments, Training, and Productivity

Another area to consider is how you determine who is to be trained and for what. This is an area that is being looked at closer by OFCCP Compliance Officers to determine whether promotional opportunities are available to all employees.

One of the safest programs you could consider is to that of assessing your employees based against your job functions as well as against those top performers performing those functions. Through an assessment program you will be able to not only identify candidates for future promotional opportunities, but plan their training activities to prepare them for those opportunities prior to actually making the promotion. Hence, they are more "up to speed" once they move into their new job.

Assessments can also be used in the hiring process as they can identify those applicants that most closely meet the attributes of your top performers on that particular job function. And assessments do this without prejudice as they are color blind and don't care about the gender of the individuals.

From the perspective of your affirmative action program assessments, used as one segment of your hiring process, can provide you with an unbiased aid in determining applicant and/or employee suitability for a specific job. The important thing to remember when using assessments or any other "tool" is that they do not become the sole criteria for making your decision.

For more information on either opinion surveys are assessments we direct you to HR Management Solutions, LLC at http://h-r-m-s.com/contact.

# APPENDICES

# Executive Order 11246, As Amended

**Executive Order 11246—Equal Employment Opportunity**

SOURCE: The provisions of Executive Order 11246 of Sept. 24, 1965, appear at 30 FR 12319, 12935, 3 CFR, 1964-1965 Comp., p.339, unless otherwise noted.

Under and by virtue of the authority vested in me as President of the United States by the Constitution and statutes of the United States, it is ordered as follows:

**Part I—Nondiscrimination in Government Employment**

[Part I superseded by EO 11478 of Aug. 8, 1969, 34 FR 12985, 3 CFR, 1966-1970 Comp., p. 803]

**Part II—Nondiscrimination in Employment by Government Contractors and Subcontractors**

**Subpart A—Duties of the Secretary of Labor**

**SEC. 201.** The Secretary of Labor shall be responsible for the administration and enforcement of Parts II and III of this Order. The Secretary shall adopt such rules and regulations and issue such orders as are deemed necessary and appropriate to achieve the purposes of Parts II and III of this Order.

[Sec. 201 amended by EO 12086 of Oct. 5, 1978, 43 FR 46501, 3 CFR, 1978 Comp., p. 230]

**Subpart B—Contractors' Agreements**

**SEC. 202.** Except in contracts exempted in accordance with Section 204 of this Order, all Government contracting agencies shall include in every Government contract hereafter entered into the following provisions:

During the performance of this contract, the contractor agrees as follows:

(1) The contractor will not discriminate against any employee or applicant for employment because of race, color, religion, sex, or national origin. The contractor will take affirmative action to ensure that applicants are employed, and that employees are treated during employment, without regard to their race, color, religion, sex or national origin. Such action shall include, but not be limited to

the following: employment, upgrading, demotion, or transfer; recruitment or recruitment advertising; layoff or termination; rates of pay or other forms of compensation; and selection for training, including apprenticeship. The contractor agrees to post in conspicuous places, available to employees and applicants for employment, notices to be provided by the contracting officer setting forth the provisions of this nondiscrimination clause.

(2) The contractor will, in all solicitations or advancements for employees placed by or on behalf of the contractor, state that all qualified applicants will receive consideration for employment without regard to race, color, religion, sex or national origin.

(3) The contractor will send to each labor union or representative of workers with which he has a collective bargaining agreement or other contract or understanding, a notice, to be provided by the agency contracting officer, advising the labor union or workers' representative of the contractor's commitments under Section 202 of Executive Order No. 11246 of September 24, 1965, and shall post copies of the notice in conspicuous places available to employees and applicants for employment.

(4) The contractor will comply with all provisions of Executive Order No. 11246 of Sept. 24, 1965, and of the rules, regulations, and relevant orders of the Secretary of Labor.

(5) The contractor will furnish all information and reports required by Executive Order No. 11246 of September 24, 1965, and by the rules, regulations, and orders of the Secretary of Labor, or pursuant thereto, and will permit access to his books, records, and accounts by the contracting agency and the Secretary of Labor for purposes of investigation to ascertain compliance with such rules, regulations, and orders.

(6) In the event of the contractor's noncompliance with the nondiscrimination clauses of this contract or with any of such rules, regulations, or orders, this contract may be cancelled, terminated, or suspended in whole or in part and the contractor may be declared ineligible for further Government contracts in accordance with procedures authorized in Executive Order No. 11246 of Sept. 24, 1965, and such other sanctions may be imposed and remedies invoked as provided in Executive Order No. 11246 of September 24, 1965, or by rule, regulation, or order of the Secretary of Labor, or as otherwise provided by law.

(7) The contractor will include the provisions of paragraphs (1) through (7) in every subcontract or purchase order unless exempted by rules, regulations, or orders of the Secretary of Labor issued pursuant to Section 204 of Executive Order No. 11246 of September 24, 1965, so that such provisions will be binding upon each subcontractor or vendor. The contractor win take such action with respect to any subcontract or purchase order as may be directed by the Secretary of Labor as a means of enforcing such provisions including sanctions for noncompliance: Provided, however, that in the event the contractor becomes involved in, or is threatened with, litigation with a subcontractor or vendor as a result of such direction, the contractor may request the United States to enter into such litigation to protect the interests of the United States." [Sec. 202 amended by EO 11375 of Oct. 13, 1967, 32 FR 14303, 3 CFR, 1966-1970 Comp., p. 684, EO 12086 of Oct. 5, 1978, 43 FR 46501, 3 CFR, 1978 Comp., p. 230]

SEC. 203. Each contractor having a contract containing the provisions prescribed in Section 202 shall file, and shall cause each of his subcontractors to file, Compliance Reports with the contracting agency or the Secretary of Labor as may be directed. Compliance Reports shall be filed within such times and shall contain such information as to the practices, policies, programs, and employment policies, programs, and employment statistics of the contractor and each subcontractor, and shall be in such form, as the Secretary of Labor may prescribe.

(b) Bidders or prospective contractors or subcontractors may be required to state whether they have participated in any previous contract subject to the provisions of this Order, or any preceding similar Executive order, and in that event to submit, on behalf of themselves and their proposed subcontractors, Compliance Reports prior to or as an initial part of their bid or negotiation of a contract.

(c) Whenever the contractor or subcontractor has a collective bargaining agreement or other contract or understanding with a labor union or an agency referring workers or providing or supervising apprenticeship or training for such workers, the Compliance Report shall include such information as to such labor union's or agency's practices and policies affecting compliance as the Secretary of Labor may prescribe: Provided, That to the extent such information is within the exclusive possession of a labor union or an agency referring workers or providing or supervising apprenticeship or training and such labor union or agency shall refuse to furnish such information to the contractor, the contractor shall so certify to the Secretary of Labor as part of its Compliance Report and shall set forth what efforts he has made to obtain such information.

(d) The Secretary of Labor may direct that any bidder or prospective contractor or subcontractor shall submit, as part of his Compliance Report, a statement in writing, signed by an authorized officer or agent on behalf of any labor union or any agency referring workers or providing or supervising apprenticeship or other training, with which the bidder or prospective contractor deals, with supporting information, to the effect that the signer's practices and policies do not discriminate on the grounds of race, color, religion, sex or national origin, and that the signer either will affirmatively cooperate in the implementation of the policy and provisions of this Order or that it consents and agrees that recruitment, employment, and the terms and conditions of employment under the proposed contract shall be in accordance with the purposes and provisions of the order. In the event that the union, or the agency shall refuse to execute such a statement, the Compliance Report shall so certify and set forth what efforts have been made to secure such a statement and such additional factual material as the Secretary of Labor may require.

[Sec. 203 amended by EO 11375 of Oct. 13, 1967, 32 FR 14303, 3 CFR, 1966-1970 Comp., p. 684; EO 12086 of Oct. 5, 1978, 43 FR 46501, 3 CFR, 1978 Comp., p. 230]

SEC. 204 (a) The Secretary of Labor may, when the Secretary deems that special circumstances in the national interest so require, exempt a contracting agency from the requirement of including any or all of the provisions of Section 202 of this **Order** in any specific contract, subcontract, or purchase **order**.

(b) The Secretary of Labor may, by rule or regulation, exempt certain classes of contracts, subcontracts, or purchase orders (1) whenever work is to be or has been performed outside the United States and no recruitment of workers within the limits of the United States is involved; (2) for standard commercial supplies or raw materials; (3) involving less than specified amounts of money or specified numbers of workers; or (4) to the extent that they involve subcontracts below a specified tier.

(c) Section 202 of this **Order** shall not apply to a Government contractor or subcontractor that is a religious corporation, association, educational institution, or society, with respect to the employment of individuals of a particular religion to perform work connected with the carrying on by such corporation, association, educational institution, or society of its activities. Such contractors and subcontractors are not exempted or excused from complying with the other requirements contained in this **Order**.

(d) The Secretary of Labor may also provide, by rule, regulation, or **order**, for the exemption of facilities of a contractor that are in all respects separate and distinct from activities of the contractor related to the performance of the contract: provided, that such an exemption will not interfere with or impede the effectuation of the purposes of this **Order**: and provided further, that in the absence of such an exemption all facilities shall be covered by the provisions of this **Order**."

[Sec. 204 amended by EO 13279 of Dec. 16, 2002, 67 FR 77141, 3 CFR, 2002 Comp., p. 77141—77144]

**Subpart C—Powers and Duties of the Secretary of Labor and the Contracting Agencies**

**SEC. 205.** The Secretary of Labor shall be responsible for securing compliance by all Government contractors and subcontractors with this Order and any implementing rules or regulations. All contracting agencies shall comply with the terms of this Order and any implementing rules, regulations, or orders of the Secretary of Labor. Contracting agencies shall cooperate with the Secretary of Labor and shall furnish such information and assistance as the Secretary may require.

[Sec. 205 amended by EO 12086 of Oct. 5, 1978, 43 FR 46501, 3 CFR, 1978 Comp., p. 230]

**SEC. 206.** The Secretary of Labor may investigate the employment practices of any Government contractor or subcontractor to determine whether or not the contractual provisions specified in Section 202 of this Order have been violated. Such investigation shall be conducted in accordance with the procedures established by the Secretary of Labor.

(b) The Secretary of Labor may receive and investigate complaints by employees or prospective employees of a Government contractor or subcontractor which allege discrimination contrary to the contractual provisions specified in Section 202 of this Order.

[Sec. 206 amended by EO 12086 of Oct. 5, 1978, 43 FR 46501, 3 CFR, 1978 Comp., p. 230]

**SEC. 207.** The Secretary of Labor shall use his/her best efforts, directly and through interested Federal, State, and local agencies, contractors, and all other available instrumentalities to cause any labor union engaged in work under Government contracts or any agency referring workers or providing or supervising apprenticeship or training for or in the course of such work to cooperate in the implementation of the purposes of this Order. The Secretary of Labor shall, in appropriate cases, notify the Equal Employment Opportunity Commission, the Department of Justice, or other appropriate Federal agencies whenever it has reason to believe that the practices of any such labor organization or agency violate Title VI or Title VII of the Civil Rights Act of 1964 or other provision of Federal law.

[Sec. 207 amended by EO 12086 of Oct. 5, 1978, 43 FR 46501, 3 CFR, 1978 Comp., p. 230]

**SEC. 208.** The Secretary of Labor, or any agency, officer, or employee in the executive branch of the Government designated by rule, regulation, or order of the Secretary, may hold such hearings, public or private, as the Secretary may deem advisable for compliance, enforcement, or educational purposes.

(b) The Secretary of Labor may hold, or cause to be held, hearings in accordance with Subsection of this Section prior to imposing, ordering, or recommending the imposition of penalties and sanctions under this Order. No order for debarment of any contractor from further Government contracts under Section 209(6) shall be made without affording the contractor an opportunity for a hearing.

**Subpart D—Sanctions and Penalties**

**SEC. 209.** In accordance with such rules, regulations, or orders as the Secretary of Labor may issue or adopt, the Secretary may:

(1) Publish, or cause to be published, the names of contractors or unions which it has concluded have complied or have failed to comply with the provisions of this Order or of the rules, regulations, and orders of the Secretary of Labor.

(2) Recommend to the Department of Justice that, in cases in which there is substantial or material violation or the threat of substantial or material violation of

the contractual provisions set forth in Section 202 of this Order, appropriate proceedings be brought to enforce those provisions, including the enjoining, within the limitations of applicable law, of organizations, individuals, or groups who prevent directly or indirectly, or seek to prevent directly or indirectly, compliance with the provisions of this Order.

(3) Recommend to the Equal Employment Opportunity Commission or the Department of Justice that appropriate proceedings be instituted under Title VII of the Civil Rights Act of 1964.

(4) Recommend to the Department of Justice that criminal proceedings be brought for the furnishing of false information to any contracting agency or to the Secretary of Labor as the case may be.

(5) After consulting with the contracting agency, direct the contracting agency to cancel, terminate, suspend, or cause to be cancelled, terminated, or suspended, any contract, or any portion or portions thereof, for failure of the contractor or subcontractor to comply with equal employment opportunity provisions of the contract. Contracts may be cancelled, terminated, or suspended absolutely or continuance of contracts may be conditioned upon a program for future compliance approved by the Secretary of Labor.

(6) Provide that any contracting agency shall refrain from entering into further contracts, or extensions or other modifications of existing contracts, with any noncomplying contractor, until such contractor has satisfied the Secretary of Labor that such contractor has established and will carry out personnel and employment policies in compliance with the provisions of this Order.

(b) Pursuant to rules and regulations prescribed by the Secretary of Labor, the Secretary shall make reasonable efforts, within a reasonable time limitation, to secure compliance with the contract provisions of this Order by methods of conference, conciliation, mediation, and persuasion before proceedings shall be instituted under subsection (a)(2) of this Section, or before a contract shall be cancelled or terminated in whole or in part under subsection (a)(5) of this Section.

[Sec. 209 amended by EO 12086 of Oct. 5, 1978, 43 FR 46501, 3 CFR, 1978 Comp., p. 230]

**SEC. 210.** Whenever the Secretary of Labor makes a determination under Section 209, the Secretary shall promptly notify the appropriate agency. The agency shall take the action directed by the Secretary and shall report the results of the action it has taken to the Secretary of Labor within such time as the Secretary shall specify. If the contracting agency fails to take the action directed within thirty days, the Secretary may take the action directly.

[Sec. 210 amended by EO 12086 of Oct. 5, 1978, 43 FR 46501, 3 CFR, 1978 Comp., p 230]

**SEC. 211.** If the Secretary shall so direct, contracting agencies shall not enter into contracts with any bidder or prospective contractor unless the bidder or prospective contractor has satisfactorily complied with the provisions of this Order or submits a program for compliance acceptable to the Secretary of Labor.

[Sec. 211 amended by EO 12086 of Oct. 5, 1978, 43 FR 46501, 3 CFR, 1978 Comp., p. 230]

**SEC. 212.** When a contract has been cancelled or terminated under Section 209(a)(5) or a contractor has been debarred from further Government contracts under Section 209(a)(6) of this Order, because of noncompliance with the contract provisions specified in Section 202 of this Order, the Secretary of Labor shall promptly notify the Comptroller General of the United States.

[Sec. 212 amended by EO 12086 of Oct. 5, 1978, 43 FR 46501, 3 CFR, 1978 Comp., p. 230]

**Subpart E—Certificates of Merit**

**SEC. 213.** The Secretary of Labor may provide for issuance of a United States Government Certificate of Merit to employers or labor unions, or other agencies which are or may hereafter be engaged in work under Government contracts, if the Secretary is satisfied that the personnel and employment practices of the employer, or that the personnel, training, apprenticeship, membership, grievance and representation, upgrading, and other practices and policies of the labor union or other agency conform to the purposes and provisions of this Order.

**SEC. 214.** Any Certificate of Merit may at any time be suspended or revoked by the Secretary of Labor if the holder thereof, in the judgment of the Secretary, has failed to comply with the provisions of this Order.

**SEC. 215.** The Secretary of Labor may provide for the exemption of any employer, labor union, or other agency from any reporting requirements imposed under or pursuant to this Order if such employer, labor union, or other agency has been awarded a Certificate of Merit which has not been suspended or revoked.

## Part III—Nondiscrimination Provisions in Federally Assisted Construction Contracts

**SEC. 301.** Each executive department and agency, which administers a program involving Federal financial assistance shall require as a condition for the approval of any grant, contract, loan, insurance, or guarantee thereunder, which may involve a construction contract, that the applicant for Federal assistance undertake and agree to incorporate, or cause to be

incorporated, into all construction contracts paid for in whole or in part with funds obtained from the Federal Government or borrowed on the credit of the Federal Government pursuant to such grant, contract, loan, insurance, or guarantee, or undertaken pursuant to any Federal program involving such grant, contract, loan, insurance, or guarantee, the provisions prescribed for Government contracts by Section 202 of this Order or such modification thereof, preserving in substance the contractor's obligations thereunder, as may be approved by the Secretary of Labor, together with such additional provisions as the Secretary deems appropriate to establish and protect the interest of the United States in the enforcement of those obligations. Each such applicant shall also undertake and agree (1) to assist and cooperate actively with the Secretary of Labor in obtaining the compliance of contractors and subcontractors with those contract provisions and with the rules, regulations and relevant orders of the Secretary, (2) to obtain and to furnish to the Secretary of Labor such information as the Secretary may require for the supervision of such compliance, (3) to carry out sanctions and penalties for violation of such obligations imposed upon contractors and subcontractors by the Secretary of Labor pursuant to Part II, Subpart D, of this Order, and (4) to refrain from entering into any contract subject to this Order, or extension or other modification of such a contract with a contractor debarred from Government contracts under Part II, Subpart D, of this Order.

[Sec. 301 amended by EO 12086 of Oct. 5, 1978, 43 FR 46501, 3 CFR, 1978 Comp., p. 230]

SEC. 302."Construction contract" as used in this Order means any contract for the construction, rehabilitation, alteration, conversion, extension, or repair of buildings, highways, or other improvements to real property.

(b) The provisions of Part II of this Order shall apply to such construction contracts, and for purposes of such application the administering department or agency shall be considered the contracting agency referred to therein.

(c) The term "applicant" as used in this Order means an applicant for Federal assistance or, as determined by agency regulation, other program participant, with respect to whom an application for any grant, contract, loan, insurance, or guarantee is not finally acted upon prior to the effective date of this Part, and it includes such an applicant after he/she becomes a recipient of such Federal assistance.

SEC. 303. The Secretary of Labor shall be responsible for obtaining the compliance of such applicants with their undertakings under this Order. Each administering department and agency is directed to cooperate with the Secretary of Labor and to furnish the Secretary such information and assistance as the Secretary may require in the performance of the Secretary's functions under this Order.

(b) In the event an applicant fails and refuses to comply with the applicant's undertakings pursuant to this Order, the Secretary of Labor may, after consulting with the administering department or agency, take any or all of the following actions: (1) direct any administering department or agency to cancel, terminate, or suspend in whole or in part the agreement, contract or other arrangement with such applicant with respect to which the failure or refusal occurred; (2) direct any administering department or agency to refrain from extending any further assistance to the applicant under the program with respect to which the failure or refusal occurred until satisfactory assurance of future compliance has been received by the Secretary of Labor from such applicant; and (3) refer the case to the Department of Justice or the Equal Employment Opportunity Commission for appropriate law enforcement or other proceedings.

(c) In no case shall action be taken with respect to an applicant pursuant to clause (1) or (2) of subsection (b) without notice and opportunity for hearing.

[Sec. 303 amended by EO 12086 of Oct. 5, 1978, 43 FR 46501, 3 CFR, 1978 Comp., p. 230]

SEC. 304. Any executive department or agency which imposes by rule, regulation, or order requirements of nondiscrimination in employment, other than requirements imposed pursuant to this Order, may delegate to the Secretary of Labor by agreement such responsibilities with respect to compliance standards, reports, and procedures as would tend to bring the administration of such requirements into conformity with the administration of requirements imposed under this Order: Provided, That actions to effect compliance by recipients of Federal financial assistance with requirements imposed pursuant to Title VI of the Civil Rights Act of 1964 shall be taken in conformity with the procedures and limitations prescribed in Section 602 thereof and the regulations of the administering department or agency issued thereunder.

### Part IV—Miscellaneous

SEC. 401. The Secretary of Labor may delegate to any officer, agency, or employee in the Executive branch of the Government, any function or duty of the Secretary under Parts II and III of this Order.

[Sec. 401 amended by EO 12086 of Oct. 5, 1978, 43 FR 46501, 3 CFR, 1978 Comp., p. 230]

SEC. 402. The Secretary of Labor shall provide administrative support for the execution of the program known as the "Plans for Progress."

SEC. 403. Executive Orders Nos. 10590 (January 19, 1955), 10722 (August 5, 1957), 10925 (March 6, 1961), 11114 (June 22, 1963), and 11162 (July 28, 1964), are hereby superseded and the President's Committee on Equal Employment Opportunity established by Executive Order No. 10925 is hereby abolished. All records and property in the custody of the Committee shall be transferred to the Office of Personnel Management and the Secretary of Labor, as appropriate.

(b) Nothing in this Order shall be deemed to relieve any person of any obligation assumed or imposed under or pursuant to any Executive Order superseded by this Order. All rules, regulations, orders, instructions, designations, and other directives issued by the President's Committee on Equal Employment Opportunity and those issued by the heads of various departments or agencies under or pursuant to any of the Executive orders superseded by this Order, shall, to the extent that they are not inconsistent with this Order, remain in full force and effect unless and until revoked or superseded by appropriate authority.

References in such directives to provisions of the superseded orders shall be deemed to be references to the comparable provisions of this Order.

[Sec. 403 amended by EO 12107 of Dec. 28, 1978, 44 FR 1055, 3 CFR, 1978 Comp., p, 264]

**SEC. 404.** The General Services Administration shall take appropriate action to revise the standard Government contract forms to accord with the provisions of this Order and of the rules and regulations of the Secretary of Labor.

**SEC. 405.** This Order shall become effective thirty days after the date of this Order.

# EO Survey

U.S. Department of Labor

Office of Federal Contract Compliance Programs
Equal Opportunity Survey
of Federal Contractor Establishments

## INTRODUCTION:

The U.S. Department of Labor, Office of Federal Contract Compliance Programs (OFCCP) is conducting this Equal Opportunity Survey (EO Survey) to obtain employment information from federal contractor establishments. We suggest that your EEO/Human Resource Director or Affirmative Action Officer be responsible for completing and/or coordinating the completion of this EO Survey.

## WHO MUST COMPLETE THE EO SURVEY

You must complete and return this Survey if both of the following statements are true:

...............Your company or corporation is
            a Federal contractor or subcontractor;
...............Your company or corporation has 50 or more employees;

....and any one of the following statements is true

...............Your company or corporation has a Federal
            contract or subcontract of $50,000 or more.
...............Your company or corporation is a financial institution
            that is an issuing agent for U.S. Savings Bonds and Notes.

................Your company or corporation serves as a
depository of Government funds in any amount.

................Your company or corporation has Government bills of lading which
in any 12-month period total or will likely total $50,000 or more.

................Your company or corporation has an open-ended or indefinite quantity
Federal contract or subcontract (such as a procurement order
or standing invoice) that will total $50,000 or more.

**Note:** Your facility may or may not be the same location where your company or
corporation is performing work under the federal contract or subcontract, but
your facility is still considered a federal contractor or subcontractor establishment. For example, Company X has a federal contract or subcontract and has
two facilities, A and B. Facility A is performing work under the federal contract
or subcontract, Facility B is not.
**Both Facility A and B of Company X are federal contractor establishments.**

**Note:** Your facility is considered a federal subcontractor establishment if it is a
subcontractor to a federal contractor and is performing work related to that contract. For example, Company X is performing work under a federal contract.
Company Y and Company Z are subcontractors of Company X. Company Y is
performing work related to Company X's federal contract. Company Z is not
performing work related to Company X's federal contract or any other federal
contract or subcontract.
**Company X and Company Y are federal subcontractor establishments;**
**Company Z is not a federal subcontractor establishment.**

> If your establishment should not complete this EO Survey, please (1) check here ☐, (2) explain in the space
> provided below why your establishment should not complete this EO Survey, and (3) sign and date the
> certification on Page 2 and return the EO Survey in the envelope provided to the address shown at right.
>
> _____
>
> _____

If your establishment should not complete this EO Survey, please (1) check here,
(2) explain in the space provided below why your establishment should not complete this EO Survey, and (3) sign and date the certification on Page 2 and return
the EO Survey in the envelope provided to the address shown at right.

## INSTRUCTIONS:

This survey has three Parts—A, B, and C. Part A is self-explanatory. Please read all instructions for parts B and C before you begin. If you have any questions, or if you need assistance in completing the EO Survey, you may call our **EO Survey Technical Assistance Help Desk at**
**1-800-397-6443** for technical assistance or the **EO Survey Policy Assistance Help Desk at**
**1-800-397-6251** for policy assistance.

## HOW TO SUBMIT THE EO SURVEY:

A pre-addressed business reply envelope is included for your convenience. Please return the entire completed and signed survey, including these instructions, **by March 26, 2004,** to:

> **EO Survey Office**
> **Office of Federal Contract Compliance Programs**
> **U.S. Department of Labor**
> **141 Canal Street**
> **Nashua, NH 03064-2879**

## DID YOU KNOW YOU CAN SUBMIT
## THE EO SURVEY *ELECTRONICALLY* ON THE WEB?

Access our electronic survey and instructions for electronic submission at **http://www.EOSURVEY.dol.gov**

## IF YOU NEED ANOTHER BLANK COPY OF THE EO SURVEY:

Contact the EO Survey Technical Assistance Help Desk at 1-800-397-6443.

## RETAIN A COMPLETED COPY OF THE EO SURVEY

You should retain a copy of your completed EO Survey. This will facilitate any discussions we may have with you should we need to call and clarify your responses.

---

---

Note: It is estimated that it will average approximately 21 hours to complete the survey. The collection of information has been approved under OMB number 1215-0196, expiration date March 31, 2005.

Send any comments concerning this burden estimate or any other aspect of this collection of information, including suggestions for reducing the burden, to the Office of Federal Contract

Compliance Programs, Room C-3325, 200 Constitution Avenue, N.W., Washington, D.C. 20210.

PERSONS ARE NOT REQUIRED TO RESPOND TO THIS COLLEC-TION OF INFORMATION UNLESS IT DISPLAYS A CURRENTLY VALID OMB NUMBER.

**OMB No. 1215-0196**
**EXPIRES:03/31/2005**

**SPECIAL TERMS YOU NEED TO KNOW TO COMPLETE THE SURVEY:**

**Certifying Officer** – An employee of your company or corporation working at this establishment that has the authority to certify the accuracy of EEO-1 Reports, Affirmative Action Programs, etc. (example: Human Resources Manager, Plant Manager, EEO Officer). The Certifying Officer should sign this EO Survey on the line indicated at right.

**Federal contracting agency** - Any department or agency in the executive branch of Government, including any wholly owned Government corporation, which enters into contracts.

**Employer Identification Number** - The 9-digit number which each corporation, partnership, or sole proprietorship has been assigned based on its application (Form SS-4) to Internal Revenue Service for an identification number.

**Applicant** – The concept of an applicant is that of a person who has indicated an interest in being considered for hiring, promotion, or other employment opportunity. This interest might be expressed by completing an application form, or might be expressed orally, depending upon the employer's practice.

**Employees** - For the purposes of this EO Survey, the term "employees" applies only to your "full time" employees, as the term "full time" is defined by your company. Do not report personnel activity or compensation data on "part time" employees, as the term "part time" is defined by your company.

**Promotion** - Any personnel action resulting in movement to a position (1) with higher pay or greater rank, or (2) requiring greater skill or responsibility, or (3) with the opportunity to attain increased pay, rank, skill, or responsibility.

**Termination** - Any separation, voluntary or involuntary, of an employee from your active or inactive payroll. A termination is a complete break in employment status.

**Annual Monetary Compensation** – An employee's base rate (wage or salary), plus other earnings such as cost-of-living allowance, hazard pay, or other increment paid to all employees regardless of tenure on the job, extrapolated and expressed in terms of a full year.

**Tenure** – Length of service; the length of time an employee has been employed by your company or corporation.

# CERTIFICATION OF EO SURVEY

*The following report is accurate and complete and was prepared in accordance with the instructions. Willfully false statements on this report are punishable by law. U.S. Code, Title 18, Section 1001.*

*Name of*
*Certifying Officer (please print):*_____

*Title:*_____

*Signature of*
*Certifying Officer:*_____

*Date:*_____

*Telephone #*
*(please include area code):*_____

*Name of Person completing*
*this EO Survey(please print):*_____

*Title:*_____

*Telephone #*
*(please include area code):*_____

## CONFIDENTIALITY:

OFCCP will treat the information you submit on this EO Survey as sensitive and confidential to the maximum extent possible under the Freedom of Information Act (FOIA), with the same disclosure safeguards that are applied to Affirmative Action Program data of a sensitive or confidential nature.

U.S. Department of Labor

Office of Federal Contract Compliance Programs
Equal Opportunity Survey
**of Federal Contractor Establishments**

## PART A—GENERAL INFORMATION

1. Your establishment's Employer Identification Number
(IRS 9-digit tax number): |__|__|__|__|__|__|__|__|__|

2. Information regarding a current Federal contract or subcontract for your corporation of at least $50,000 (*You may report any current Federal contract or subcontract of at least $50,000).*

   **If You are a Federal Contractor:**

   a. Name of Federal contracting agency:
   _____

   b. Contract number:
   #_____

   **If You are a Federal Subcontractor:**

   c. Name of Prime contractor:
   _____

   d. Contract number:
   #_____

3. Expiration date of your establishment's current Affirmative Action Program(s) addressing:

a. Race, color, religion, sex, national origin
(please enter date in MM/DD/YY format): ___/___/___

If you do not know the expiration date, check this box————————

If your establishment does not have this document,
check this box————————————————————

b. Individuals with disabilities
(please enter date in MM/DD/YY format): ___/___/___

If you do not know the expiration date, check this box————————

If your establishment does not have this document,
check this box————————————————————

c. Vietnam Era, special disabled, and other protected veterans (please enter
date in MM/DD/YY format): ___/___/___
If you do not know the expiration date, check this box————————

If your establishment does not have this document,
check this box————————————————————--

4. Did your establishment list any employment openings with the local office of
your state employment service and/or America's Job Bank during the period
January 1 through December 31 of the most recently concluded calendar year, or
during the 12-month period covered by your most recently concluded Affirmative
Action Program (AAP) year, if it does not coincide with the calendar year?

No employment openings were listed————————————————

No employment openings were listed,
but all employment openings were either
positions filled from within, executive
and top management positions, or positions
for 3 days employment or less————————————————

Yes, employment openings were listed————————————————————

If yes, how many employment openings were listed?————[_____]

5. If your address or other identifying information on the mailing label was incorrect, please provide the corrected information below:

Establishment:_____

Street Address or P.O. Box:_____

_____

City, State, Zip Code:_____

EEO-1 Number for this establishment:_____

Note: For complete guidance, refer to Executive Order 11246, as amended and its implementing regulations at 41 CFR Parts 60-1 through 60-50; Section 503 of the Rehabilitation Act of 1973, as amended and its implementing regulations at 41 CFR Part 60-741; and 38 U.S.C. 4212, the Vietnam Era Veterans' Readjustment Assistance Act of 1974 (VEVRAA), as amended and its implementing regulations at 41 CFR Part 60-250.

# INSTRUCTIONS FOR PART B:

WHO TO REPORT ON: Part B information should include applicant, hiring, promotion, termination, and incumbency data for <u>"full time" employees only</u>, however the term "full time" is defined by your company.

TIME FRAME FOR REPORTING: Part B information should report on personnel activity covering your choice of one of the following two time frames:

(1) The period January 1 through December 31, 2003, or

(2) The 12-month period covered by your most recently concluded Affirmative Action Program (AAP) year, if it does not coincide with the calendar year (for example, April 1, 2002 through March 31, 2003).

<u>Regardless of which of the above time frames you wish to use, all Part B information must cover the same time frame.</u>

Based on your choice of time frames, please report Applicants, Hires, Promotions, and Terminations for January 1 through December 31, 2003, or for the 12-month period covered by your most recently concluded AAP year. Please report "Employees" as of December 31, 2003, or the last day of the most recently concluded AAP year.

EEO-1 CATEGORY: For each personnel activity identified, fill in the total number for the action indicated, by gender, race, and ethnicity and EEO-1 category. The EEO-1 categories are: <u>(1) Officials & Managers; (2) Professionals; (3) Technicians; (4) Sales Workers; (5) Office & Clerical; (6) Craft Workers; (7) Operatives; (8) Laborers; (9) Service Workers</u>. All employees reported in "Full Time Employees At End Of Year (Calendar or AAP)" on Page 9 in Part B of this EO Survey must be accounted for and reported on in Part C.

WHAT TO REPORT—PERSONNEL ACTIVITY

<u>Applicants</u>—Please indicate the number of applicants for "full time" positions by gender, race, and ethnicity, sorted by EEO-1 category, for the period of January

1 through December 31, 2003, or for the 12-month period covered by your most recently concluded AAP year.

**Hires**—Please indicate the number of hires for "full time" positions by gender, race, and ethnicity, sorted by EEO-1 category, for the period of January 1 through December 31, 2003, or for the 12-month period covered by your most recently concluded AAP year. Do not include non-competitive transfers from other facilities of your company or establishment.

**Promotions**—Please indicate the number of promotions of "full time" employees by gender, race, and ethnicity, sorted by EEO-1 category, for the period of January 1 through December 31, 2003, or for the
12-month period covered by your most recently concluded AAP year. Report the number of promotions within the EEO-1 category where it occurred, however, in instances where there are promotions from one EEO-1 category to another EEO-1 category, report those promotions in the EEO-1 category the individual was promoted into. For example, a person who is promoted from a junior engineer to a senior engineer would be counted as a promotion within the "Professional" EEO-1 category. A person promoted from a senior engineer to a manager would be counted as a promotion into the "Officials and Managers" EEO-1 category.

**Terminations**—Please indicate the number of terminations of "full time" employees by gender, race, and ethnicity, sorted by EEO-1 category, for the period of January 1 through December 31, 2003, or for the 12-month period covered by your most recently concluded AAP year. Include voluntary and involuntary terminations.

**Employees at end of Calendar/AAP Year**—Please indicate the number of incumbent "full time" employees by gender, race, and ethnicity, sorted by EEO-1 category, as of December 31, 2003, or the last day of the most recently concluded AAP year.

ABOUT RACE/ETHNIC IDENTIFICATION FOR PART B-You may acquire race/ethnic information necessary for this survey either by visual observation of the work force, or from employment records. If you maintain records, we recommend that you keep them separately from the employee's basic personnel file or other records available to those responsible for personnel decisions. Since OFCCP permits visual observations, the fact that race/ethnic identifications are not present on employment records is not an excuse for omitting the data we request.

*Note: The following reflects OMB guidelines regarding the recording and reporting of Hispanic or Latino ethnicity separately from the recording and reporting of racial data, and the establishment of "Native Hawaiian or Other Pacific Islander" as a separate racial category. For the purposes of this Survey only, you may submit data in either of the formats listed below (as FORMAT 1 and FORMAT 2).*

FORMAT 1: Complete Part B using the following categories. Although persons may identify with more than one racial category, for this EO Survey count each person only once:

American Indian or Alaskan Native—A person having origins in any of the original peoples of North America and South America (including Central America), and who maintains tribal affiliation or community attachment.

Asian—A person having origins in any of the original peoples of the Far East, Southeast Asia, or the Indian subcontinent including, for example, Cambodia, China, India, Japan, Korea, Malaysia, Pakistan, the Philippine Islands, Thailand, and Vietnam.

Black or African American—A person having origins in any of the Black racial groups of Africa. Terms such as "Haitian" or "Negro" can be used in addition to "Black or African American."

Native Hawaiian or Other Pacific Islander—A person having origins in any of the original peoples of Hawaii, Guam, Samoa, or other Pacific Islands.

White—A person having origins in any of the original peoples of Europe, North Africa, or the Middle East.

Hispanic or Latino (All races)—A person of Mexican, Puerto Rican, Cuban, Central or South American, or other Spanish culture or origin, regardless of race.

**Hispanic or Latino (White race only)**—A person of Mexican, Puerto Rican, Cuban, Central or South American, or other Spanish culture or origin, and of the White race.

**Hispanic or Latino (all other races)**—A person of Mexican, Puerto Rican, Cuban, Central or South American, or other Spanish culture or origin, and of any race other than White.

**Race missing or unknown**—Applies to **Applicants only**, where a resume or application that is screened is received without any racial or ethnic identification and no further contact is made with the applicant.

FORMAT 2: This is the same format as FORMAT 1, above, except:

• Record all actions pertaining to Hispanics or Latinos in the "**Hispanic or Latino (all races)**" columns on pages 5, 6, 7, 8, and 9 of this EO Survey.

• **Leave the "Hispanic or Latino (White)" and "Hispanic and Latino (all other races)" columns blank on pages 5, 6, 7, 8, and 9 of this EO Survey.**

• Record all actions pertaining to Asians, Hawaiians, and Other Pacific Islanders in the "**Asian**" columns on pages 5, 6, 7, 8, and 9 of this EO Survey.

• **Leave the "Native Hawaiian or Other Pacific Islander" columns blank on pages 5, 6, 7, 8, and 9 of this EO Survey.**

## PART B—PERSONNEL ACTIVITY BY EEO-1 CATEGORY—APPLICANTS

Time Frame: (check one):

—The following personnel activity covers the period January 1 through December 31, 2003

—The following personnel activity covers the most recently concluded Affirmative Action Program year, which is not January 1 through December 31, 2003

| OFFICIALS/MANAGERS | American Indian or Alaska Native | Asian | Black or African American | Native Hawaiian or Other Pacific Islander | White | HispanicorLatino (all races) | Hispanic or Latino (White race only) | Hispanic or Latino (all other races) | Race unknown |
|---|---|---|---|---|---|---|---|---|---|
| Male | | | | | | | | | |
| Female | | | | | | | | | |
| PROFESSIONALS | American Indian or Alaska Native | Asian | Black or African American | Native Hawaiian or Other Pacific Islander | White | HispanicorLatino (all races) | Hispanic or Latino (White race only) | Hispanic or Latino (all other races) | Race unknown |
| Male | | | | | | | | | |
| Female | | | | | | | | | |
| TECHNICIANS | American Indian or Alaska Native | Asian | Black or African American | Native Hawaiian or Other Pacific Islander | White | HispanicorLatino (all races) | Hispanic or Latino (White race only) | Hispanic or Latino (all other races) | Race unknown |
| Male | | | | | | | | | |
| Female | | | | | | | | | |
| SALES WORKERS | American Indian or Alaska Native | Asian | Black or African American | Native Hawaiian or Other Pacific Islander | White | HispanicorLatino (all races) | Hispanic or Latino (White race only) | Hispanic or Latino (all other races) | Race unknown |
| Male | | | | | | | | | |
| Female | | | | | | | | | |
| OFFICE AND CLERICAL | American Indian or Alaska Native | Asian | Black or African American | Native Hawaiian or Other Pacific Islander | White | HispanicorLatino (all races) | Hispanic or Latino (White race only) | Hispanic or Latino (all other races) | Race unknown |
| Male | | | | | | | | | |
| Female | | | | | | | | | |
| CRAFT WORKERS | American Indian or Alaska Native | Asian | Black or African American | Native Hawaiian or Other Pacific Islander | White | HispanicorLatino (all races) | Hispanic or Latino (White race only) | Hispanic or Latino (all other races) | Race unknown |
| Male | | | | | | | | | |
| Female | | | | | | | | | |
| OPERATIVES | American Indian or Alaska Native | Asian | Black or African American | Native Hawaiian or Other Pacific Islander | White | HispanicorLatino (all races) | Hispanic or Latino (White race only) | Hispanic or Latino (all other races) | ce unknown |
| Male | | | | | | | | | |
| Female | | | | | | | | | |
| LABORERS | American Indian or Alaska Native | Asian | Black or African American | Native Hawaiian or Other Pacific Islander | White | HispanicorLatino (all races) | Hispanic or Latino (White race only) | Hispanic or Latino (all other races) | Race unknown |
| Male | | | | | | | | | |
| Female | | | | | | | | | |
| SERVICE WORKERS | American Indian or Alaska Native | Asian | Black or African American | Native Hawaiian or Other Pacific Islander | White | HispanicorLatino (all races) | Hispanic or Latino (White race only) | Hispanic or Latino (all other races) | Race unknown |
| Male | | | | | | | | | |
| Female | | | | | | | | | |

## PART B—PERSONNEL ACTIVITY BY EEO-1 CATEGORY—HIRES

For Time Frame as Specified on Page 5 in Part B of this EO Survey

| OFFICIALS AND MANAGERS | American Indian or Alaska Native | Asian | Black or African American | Native Hawaiian or Other Pacific Islander | White | Hispanic or Latino (all races) | Hispanic or Latino (White race only) | Hispanic or Latino (all other races) |
|---|---|---|---|---|---|---|---|---|
| Male | | | | | | | | |
| Female | | | | | | | | |

| PROFESSIONALS | American Indian or Alaska Native | Asian | Black or African American | Native Hawaiian or Other Pacific Islander | White | Hispanic or Latino (all races) | Hispanic or Latino (White race only) | Hispanic or Latino (all other races) |
|---|---|---|---|---|---|---|---|---|
| Male | | | | | | | | |
| Female | | | | | | | | |

| TECHNICIANS | American Indian or Alaska Native | Asian | Black or African American | Native Hawaiian or Other Pacific Islander | White | Hispanic or Latino (all races) | Hispanic or Latino (White race only) | Hispanic or Latino (all other races) |
|---|---|---|---|---|---|---|---|---|
| Male | | | | | | | | |
| Female | | | | | | | | |

| SALES WORKERS | American Indian or Alaska Native | Asian | Black or African American | Native Hawaiian or Other Pacific Islander | White | Hispanic or Latino (all races) | Hispanic or Latino (White race only) | Hispanic or Latino (all other races) |
|---|---|---|---|---|---|---|---|---|
| Male | | | | | | | | |
| Female | | | | | | | | |

| OFFICE AND CLERICAL | American Indian or Alaska Native | Asian | Black or African American | Native Hawaiian or Other Pacific Islander | White | Hispanic or Latino (all races) | Hispanic or Latino (White race only) | Hispanic or Latino (all other races) |
|---|---|---|---|---|---|---|---|---|
| Male | | | | | | | | |
| Female | | | | | | | | |

| CRAFT WORKERS | American Indian or Alaska Native | Asian | Black or African American | Native Hawaiian or Other Pacific Islander | White | Hispanic or Latino (all races) | Hispanic or Latino (White race only) | Hispanic or Latino (all other races) |
|---|---|---|---|---|---|---|---|---|
| Male | | | | | | | | |
| Female | | | | | | | | |

| OPERATIVES | American Indian or Alaska Native | Asian | Black or African American | Native Hawaiian or Other Pacific Islander | White | Hispanic or Latino (all races) | Hispanic or Latino (White race only) | Hispanic or Latino (all other races) |
|---|---|---|---|---|---|---|---|---|
| Male | | | | | | | | |
| Female | | | | | | | | |

| LABORERS | American Indian or Alaska Native | Asian | Black or African American | Native Hawaiian or Other Pacific Islander | White | Hispanic or Latino (all races) | Hispanic or Latino (White race only) | Hispanic or Latino (all other races) |
|---|---|---|---|---|---|---|---|---|
| Male | | | | | | | | |
| Female | | | | | | | | |

| SERVICE WORKERS | American Indian or Alaska Native | Asian | Black or African American | Native Hawaiian or Other Pacific Islander | White | Hispanic or Latino (all races) | Hispanic or Latino (White race only) | Hispanic or Latino (all other races) |
|---|---|---|---|---|---|---|---|---|
| Male | | | | | | | | |
| Female | | | | | | | | |

# PART B—PERSONNEL ACTIVITY BY EEO-1 CATEGORY—PROMOTIONS
For Time Frame as Specified on Page 5 in Part B of this EO Survey

| *OFFICIALS AND MANAGERS* | American Indian or Alaska Native | Asian | Black or African American | Native Hawaiian or Other Pacific Islander | White | HispanicorLatino (all races) | Hispanic or Latino (White race only) | Hispanic or Latino (all other races) |
|---|---|---|---|---|---|---|---|---|
| Male | | | | | | | | |
| Female | | | | | | | | |

| *PROFESSIONALS* | American Indian or Alaska Native | Asian | Black or African American | Native Hawaiian or Other Pacific Islander | White | HispanicorLatino (all races) | Hispanic or Latino (White race only) | Hispanic or Latino (all other races) |
|---|---|---|---|---|---|---|---|---|
| Male | | | | | | | | |
| Female | | | | | | | | |

| *TECHNICIANS* | American Indian or Alaska Native | Asian | Black or African American | Native Hawaiian or Other Pacific Islander | White | HispanicorLatino (all races) | Hispanic or Latino (White race only) | Hispanic or Latino (all other races) |
|---|---|---|---|---|---|---|---|---|
| Male | | | | | | | | |
| Female | | | | | | | | |

| *SALES WORKERS* | American Indian or Alaska Native | Asian | Black or African American | Native Hawaiian or Other Pacific Islander | White | HispanicorLatino (all races) | Hispanic or Latino (White race only) | Hispanic or Latino (all other races) |
|---|---|---|---|---|---|---|---|---|
| Male | | | | | | | | |
| Female | | | | | | | | |

| *OFFICE AND CLERICAL* | American Indian or Alaska Native | Asian | Black or African American | Native Hawaiian or Other Pacific Islander | White | HispanicorLatino (all races) | Hispanic or Latino (White race only) | Hispanic or Latino (all other races) |
|---|---|---|---|---|---|---|---|---|
| Male | | | | | | | | |
| Female | | | | | | | | |

| *CRAFT WORKERS* | American Indian or Alaska Native | Asian | Black or African American | Native Hawaiian or Other Pacific Islander | White | HispanicorLatino (all races) | Hispanic or Latino (White race only) | Hispanic or Latino (all other races) |
|---|---|---|---|---|---|---|---|---|
| Male | | | | | | | | |
| Female | | | | | | | | |

| *OPERATIVES* | American Indian or Alaska Native | Asian | Black or African American | Native Hawaiian or Other Pacific Islander | White | HispanicorLatino (all races) | Hispanic or Latino (White race only) | Hispanic or Latino (all other races) |
|---|---|---|---|---|---|---|---|---|
| Male | | | | | | | | |
| Female | | | | | | | | |

| *LABORERS* | American Indian or Alaska Native | Asian | Black or African American | Native Hawaiian or Other Pacific Islander | White | HispanicorLatino (all races) | Hispanic or Latino (White race only) | Hispanic or Latino (all other races) |
|---|---|---|---|---|---|---|---|---|
| Male | | | | | | | | |
| Female | | | | | | | | |

| *SERVICE WORKERS* | American Indian or Alaska Native | Asian | Black or African American | Native Hawaiian or Other Pacific Islander | White | HispanicorLatino (all races) | Hispanic or Latino (White race only) | Hispanic or Latino (all other races) |
|---|---|---|---|---|---|---|---|---|
| Male | | | | | | | | |
| Female | | | | | | | | |

## PART B—PERSONNEL ACTIVITY BY EEO-1 CATEGORY—TERMINATIONS
### For Time Frame as Specified on Page 5 in Part B of this EO Survey

| OFFICIALS AND MANAGERS | American Indian or Alaska Native | Asian | Black or African American | Native Hawaiian or Other Pacific Islander | White | HispanicorLatino (all races) | Hispanic or Latino (White race only) | Hispanic or Latino (all other races) |
|---|---|---|---|---|---|---|---|---|
| Male | | | | | | | | |
| Female | | | | | | | | |
| PROFESSIONALS | American Indian or Alaska Native | Asian | Black or African American | Native Hawaiian or Other Pacific Islander | White | HispanicorLatino (all races) | Hispanic or Latino (White race only) | Hispanic or Latino (all other races) |
| Male | | | | | | | | |
| Female | | | | | | | | |
| TECHNICIANS | American Indian or Alaska Native | Asian | Black or African American | Native Hawaiian or Other Pacific Islander | White | HispanicorLatino (all races) | Hispanic or Latino (White race only) | Hispanic or Latino (all other races) |
| Male | | | | | | | | |
| Female | | | | | | | | |
| SALES WORKERS | American Indian or Alaska Native | Asian | Black or African American | Native Hawaiian or Other Pacific Islander | White | HispanicorLatino (all races) | Hispanic or Latino (White race only) | Hispanic or Latino (all other races) |
| Male | | | | | | | | |
| Female | | | | | | | | |
| OFFICE AND CLERICAL | American Indian or Alaska Native | Asian | Black or African American | Native Hawaiian or Other Pacific Islander | White | HispanicorLatino (all races) | Hispanic or Latino (White race only) | Hispanic or Latino (all other races) |
| Male | | | | | | | | |
| Female | | | | | | | | |
| CRAFT WORKERS | American Indian or Alaska Native | Asian | Black or African American | Native Hawaiian or Other Pacific Islander | White | HispanicorLatino (all races) | Hispanic or Latino (White race only) | Hispanic or Latino (all other races) |
| Male | | | | | | | | |
| Female | | | | | | | | |
| OPERATIVES | American Indian or Alaska Native | Asian | Black or African American | Native Hawaiian or Other Pacific Islander | White | HispanicorLatino (all races) | Hispanic or Latino (White race only) | Hispanic or Latino (all other races) |
| Male | | | | | | | | |
| Female | | | | | | | | |
| LABORERS | American Indian or Alaska Native | Asian | Black or African American | Native Hawaiian or Other Pacific Islander | White | HispanicorLatino (all races) | Hispanic or Latino (White race only) | Hispanic or Latino (all other races) |
| Male | | | | | | | | |
| Female | | | | | | | | |
| SERVICE WORKERS | American Indian or Alaska Native | Asian | Black or African American | Native Hawaiian or Other Pacific Islander | White | HispanicorLatino (all races) | Hispanic or Latino (White race only) | Hispanic or Latino (all other races) |
| Male | | | | | | | | |
| Female | | | | | | | | |

# PART B—PERSONNEL ACTIVITY BY EEO-1 CATEGORY—FULL TIME EMPLOYEES AT END OF YEAR (CALENDAR OR AAP)

For Time Frame as Specified on Page 5 in Part B of this EO Survey

| OFFICIALS AND MANAGERS | American Indian or Alaska Native | Asian | Black or African American | Native Hawaiian or Other Pacific Islander | White | HispanicorLatino (all races) | Hispanic or Latino (White race only) | Hispanic or Latino (all other races) |
|---|---|---|---|---|---|---|---|---|
| Male | | | | | | | | |
| Female | | | | | | | | |
| PROFESSIONALS | American Indian or Alaska Native | Asian | Black or African American | Native Hawaiian or Other Pacific Islander | White | HispanicorLatino (all races) | Hispanic or Latino (White race only) | Hispanic or Latino (all other races) |
| Male | | | | | | | | |
| Female | | | | | | | | |
| TECHNICIANS | American Indian or Alaska Native | Asian | Black or African American | Native Hawaiian or Other Pacific Islander | White | HispanicorLatino (all races) | Hispanic or Latino (White race only) | Hispanic or Latino (all other races) |
| Male | | | | | | | | |
| Female | | | | | | | | |
| SALES WORKERS | American Indian or Alaska Native | Asian | Black or African American | Native Hawaiian or Other Pacific Islander | White | HispanicorLatino (all races) | Hispanic or Latino (White race only) | Hispanic or Latino (all other races) |
| Male | | | | | | | | |
| Female | | | | | | | | |
| OFFICE AND CLERICAL | American Indian or Alaska Native | Asian | Black or African American | Native Hawaiian or Other Pacific Islander | White | HispanicorLatino (all races) | Hispanic or Latino (White race only) | Hispanic or Latino (all other races) |
| Male | | | | | | | | |
| Female | | | | | | | | |
| CRAFT WORKERS | American Indian or Alaska Native | Asian | Black or African American | Native Hawaiian or Other Pacific Islander | White | HispanicorLatino (all races) | Hispanic or Latino (White race only) | Hispanic or Latino (all other races) |
| Male | | | | | | | | |
| Female | | | | | | | | |
| OPERATIVES | American Indian or Alaska Native | Asian | Black or African American | Native Hawaiian or Other Pacific Islander | White | HispanicorLatino (all races) | Hispanic or Latino (White race only) | Hispanic or Latino (all other races) |
| Male | | | | | | | | |
| Female | | | | | | | | |
| LABORERS | American Indian or Alaska Native | Asian | Black or African American | Native Hawaiian or Other Pacific Islander | White | HispanicorLatino (all races) | Hispanic or Latino (White race only) | Hispanic or Latino (all other races) |
| Male | | | | | | | | |
| Female | | | | | | | | |
| SERVICE WORKERS | American Indian or Alaska Native | Asian | Black or African American | Native Hawaiian or Other Pacific Islander | White | HispanicorLatino (all races) | Hispanic or Latino (White race only) | Hispanic or Latino (all other races) |
| Male | | | | | | | | |
| Female | | | | | | | | |

## INSTRUCTIONS FOR PART C:

**WHO TO REPORT ON:** In order for your EO Survey to be considered a valid submission Part C <u>must</u> contain annual monetary compensation and tenure data for all employees listed as **"Full Time Employees At End Of Year (Calendar or AAP)"** on Page 9 in Part B of this EO Survey, and it <u>must not</u> include monetary compensation and tenure data for anyone else.

**TIME FRAME FOR REPORTING:** The time frame is December 31, 2003, or the last day of the most recently concluded AAP year, whichever you chose for reporting on Page 9, Part B of this EO Survey.

**MINORITY/NON-MINORITY:** Employees are to be grouped and reported in four groups: **minority female, non-minority female, minority male, and non-minority male employees.** For the purposes of this EO Survey, a "non-minority" is defined as someone of the White race who is not of Hispanic (or Latino) ethnicity. A "minority" is defined as all races other than White or someone of the White race who is of Hispanic (or Latino) ethnicity, or someone who has reported more than one race.

**EEO-1 CATEGORY:** Employees are also to be sorted by EEO-1 category. The EEO-1 categories are: <u>(1) **Officials & Managers;** (2) **Professionals;** (3) Technicians; (4) Sales Workers; (5) Office & Clerical; (6) Craft Workers; (7) Operatives; (8) Laborers; (9) Service Workers</u>.

**In order for your EO Survey to be considered a valid submission all end-of-year employees reported in "Full Time Employees At End Of Year (Calendar or AAP)" on Page 9 in Part B of this EO Survey must be accounted for and reported on in Part C.**

**WHAT TO REPORT—ANNUAL MONETARY COMPENSATION:** For the purposes of this EO Survey, annual monetary compensation is defined as an employee's base rate (wage or salary), plus other earnings such as cost-of-living allowance, hazard pay, or other increment paid to all employees regardless of tenure on the job. Annual monetary compensation should not include the value of benefits, overtime, or one-time payments such as relocation expenses. Annual monetary compensation should be expressed in terms of an annual amount.

Report total annual monetary compensation information for all employees reported in **"Full Time Employees At End Of Year (Calendar or AAP)" on Page 9 in Part B of this EO Survey**. While all annual monetary compensation figures should be expressed in terms of a full year, please note that this figure *may not reflect an employee's actual earnings for a year.* For those employees who have worked less than a full year, (e.g., those employees hired within the last year), please project (extrapolate) their hourly or weekly rate to compute an annual rate.

**WHAT TO REPORT—TENURE:** For the purposes of this EO Survey, tenure is defined as the length of time an employee has been with your company.

For each relevant EEO-1 category please indicate:

Total Annual Monetary Compensation for All Employees—**Please indicate the annual monetary compensation earned by "full time" minority females, non-minority females, minority males, and non-minority males within each EEO-1 category**. Include only those employees reported in "Full Time Employees At End Of Year (Calendar or AAP)" on Page 9 in Part B of this EO Survey.

**Lowest Annual Monetary Compensation of any Single Employee**—From the figures used to compute the Total Annual Monetary Compensation above, please indicate the lowest single annual monetary compensation among "full time" minority females, non-minority females, minority males, and non-minority males within each EEO-1 category. **Include only those employees reported in "Full Time Employees At End Of Year (Calendar or AAP)" on Page 9 in Part B of this EO Survey.**

**Highest Annual Monetary Compensation of any Single Employee**—From the figures used to compute the Total Annual Monetary Compensation above, please indicate the highest single annual monetary compensation among "full time" incumbent minority females, non-minority females, minority males, and non-minority males within each EEO-1 category. **Include only those employees reported in "Full Time Employees At End Of Year (Calendar or AAP)" on Page 9 in Part B of this EO Survey.**

**Average Tenure of Employees with Firm**—Please indicate the average length of time, in years and months, that "full time" incumbent **minority females, non-minority females, minority males, and non-minority males** within each EEO-1 category. **Include only those employees reported in "Full Time Employees At End Of Year (Calendar or AAP)" on Page 9 in Part B of this EO Survey.**

# PART C—COMPENSATION DATA BY EEO-1 CATEGORY

Annual Monetary Compensation and Tenure Data by EEO-1 Category for Employees reported in "FULL TIME EMPLOYEES AT END OF YEAR (CALENDAR OR AAP)" on Page 9 in Part B of this EO Survey

Check one:

—The following compensation data covers full time employees as of December 31, 2003

—The following compensation data covers full time employees as of the most recently concluded Affirmative Action Program year, which is not January 1 through December 31, 2003

| | MINORITY FEMALES | | | | NON-MINORITY FEMALES | | | |
|---|---|---|---|---|---|---|---|---|
| | Total Annual Monetary Compensation for All Minority Female Employees | Lowest Annual Monetary Compensation of any Single Minority Female Employee | Highest Annual Monetary Compensation of any Single Minority Female Employee | Average Tenure of Minority Female Employees with Firm YEARS MONTHS | Total Annual Monetary Compensation for All Non-Minority Female Employees | Lowest Annual Monetary Compensation of any Single Non-Minority Female Employee | Highest Annual Monetary Compensation of any Single Non-Minority Female Employee | Average Tenure of Non-Minority Female Employees with Firm YEARS MONTHS |
| OFFICIALS AND MANAGERS | | | | | | | | |
| PROFESSIONALS | | | | | | | | |
| TECHNICIANS | | | | | | | | |
| SALES WORKERS | | | | | | | | |
| OFFICE AND CLERICAL | | | | | | | | |
| CRAFT WORKERS | | | | | | | | |
| OPERATIVES | | | | | | | | |
| LABORERS | | | | | | | | |
| SERVICE WORKERS | | | | | | | | |

## PART C—COMPENSATION DATA BY EEO-1 CATEGORY

Annual Monetary Compensation and Tenure Data by EEO-1 Category for Employees reported in "FULL TIME EMPLOYEES AT END OF YEAR (CALENDAR OR AAP)" on Page 9 in Part B of this EO Survey

| | MINORITY MALES | | | | | NON MINORITY MALES | | | | |
|---|---|---|---|---|---|---|---|---|---|---|
| | Total Annual Monetary Compensation for All Minority Male Employees | Lowest Annual Monetary Compensation of any Single Minority Male Employee | Highest Annual Monetary Compensation of any Single Minority Male Employee | Average Tenure of Minority Male Employees with Firm YEARS MONTHS | | Total Annual Monetary Compensation for All Non-Minority Male Employees | Lowest Annual Monetary Compensation of any Single Non-Minority Male Employee | Highest Annual Monetary Compensation of any Single Non-Minority Male Employee | Average Tenure of Non-Minority Male Employees with Firm YEARS MONTHS | |
| OFFICIALS AND MANAGERS | | | | | | | | | | |
| PROFESSIONALS | | | | | | | | | | |
| TECHNICIANS | | | | | | | | | | |
| SALES WORKERS | | | | | | | | | | |
| OFFICE AND CLERICAL | | | | | | | | | | |
| CRAFT WORKERS | | | | | | | | | | |
| OPERATIVES | | | | | | | | | | |
| LABORERS | | | | | | | | | | |
| SERVICE WORKERS | | | | | | | | | | |

# Compliance Scheduling Letter

August 19, 2004
COMPANY NAME

Dear Federal Contractor:

The U.S. Department of Labor, Office of Federal Contract Compliance Programs (OFCCP) is informing you that one or more of your establishments have been selected for potential scheduling of a compliance review under the Federal Contractor Selection System (FCSS), formerly referred to as the Equal Employment Data System (EEDS). This letter provides a listing of the selected establishments which you can forward to the identified establishments and to the pertinent management officials of any business entities affiliated with the establishments listed in this letter. As each establishment is scheduled for a review we will provide the establishment with notice under established OFCCP scheduling procedures; this is not a scheduling letter.

As of July 2004, the OFCCP designed and implemented a new FCSS. The new system for this cycle selected 3,560 establishments for possible compliance reviews. At this time, OFCCP anticipates that reviews will be scheduled for all selected establishments within the next 12 months; however, based on the findings from these reviews and available resources, some of these reviews may not occur until later or will be dropped from the scheduling list for this cycle. When we have completed this cycle, we will inform you of any new selections in a similar manner and any additional changes in the selection process. Questions about the compliance review process should be directed to your regional OFCCP office. Contact information and compliance assistance information can be found at the OFCCP Compliance Assistance Calendar Web PageBhttp://www.dol.gov/esa/ofccp/Calendars/caevents.htm and the OFCCP Compliance Assistance Web Page Link B http://www.dol.gov/esa/regs/compliance/ofccp/ofcpcomp.htm

The new FCSS replaces the prior EEDS methodology in an effort to improve the accuracy of the selection process and to reduce the burden to larger multi-establishment contractors. The new system is considered by the OFCCP to be a trial system that is subject to change in future cycles of the FCSS based on new and existing research studies. The system is based on external research conducted by Westat, a firm recognized for their expertise in data collection and analysis. Unlike prior OFCCP systems that were developed internally by OFCCP without the benefit of a systematic study, the new system draws upon Westat's thorough analysis of data from ten years of OFCCP compliance reviews. Westat used such data to formally identify and characterize relationships between reported EEO-1 workforce profiles and historical OFCCP findings of discrimination. Specifically, the new model compares the workforce profile of contractor establishments to others in the same industry and to the profile of the local labor market supply as obtained from 2000 Census data. We have applied the Westat mathematical model that defines these relationships to basically rank contractor establishments on their likelihood of discrimination. In comparison to the prior EEDS methodology, our initial analysis and that from Westat indicates that the new model should be substantially better in targeting establishments with discrimination. To validate the model, we plan to conduct compliance reviews under the new FCSS starting with a pilot sample of approximately 700 top ranked establishments, assess the system, and proceed accordingly.

The new system also addresses problems with simultaneous, multiple compliance reviews arising out of the recent and significant increase in the number of compliance reviews scheduled by OFCCP. Under the new system, we have limited the number of establishments per contractor to be scheduled per year to no more than 25. For this cycle, and to the extent possible, we will attempt to limit reviews among corporate affiliated establishments to 25 including any reviews that were open as of March 2004. We have staggered the scheduling process so that several reviews are not conducted at the same point in time for any corporations with mulitple establishments. Lastly, OFCCP will give serious consideration to any remedial action voluntarily undertaken by that particular establishment prior to the conduct of an OFCCP review for both small and large contractors where compliance deficiencies have been identified through self-audits conducted by any of our establishments. Such remedial action may mitigate any relief sought by OFCCP, to the extent the remedial action completely corrects the problem(s) at issue.

Sincerely,


Charles E. James Sr.
Deputy Assistant Secretary
For Federal Contract Compliance

# POLICY STATEMENT

41 CFR 60—741.44(a)
41 CFR 60—250.44(a)

It is the policy of XYZ Company to encourage and support equal employment opportunity for all employees and applicants for employment without regard to sex, race, color, ancestry, religious creed, national origin, physical disability, mental disability, age, marital status, disabled veteran or Vietnam era veteran status. Employment decisions will be evaluated on the basis of an individual's skills, knowledge, abilities, job performance, and other legitimate qualifications, and where appropriate in promotion and transfers, seniority. Equal Employment Opportunity is among the very highest priorities for XYZ Company.

Employees and applicants shall not be subjected to harassment, intimidation, threats, coercion, or discrimination because they have engaged in or may engage in any of the following activities:

1. Filing a complaint;
2. Assisting or participating in an investigation, compliance review, hearing, or any other activity related to the administration of section 503 of the Rehabilitation Act of 1973, as amended (section 503), the Vietnam Era Veterans' Readjustment Assistance Act of 1974, as amended (VEVRRA) or any other Federal, State, or local law requiring equal opportunity for disabled persons, special disabled veterans, veterans of the Vietnam era, or other eligible veterans;
3. Opposing any act or practice made unlawful by section 503, VEVRRA or their implementing regulations or any other Federal, State, or local law requiring equal opportunity for disabled persons, special disabled veterans, veterans of the Vietnam era, or other eligible veterans;
4. Exercising any other right protected by section 503, VEVRRA or their implementing regulations.

Affirmative action and equal employment opportunity affects all employment practices at XYZ Company including recruiting, hiring, transfer, promotion, training, compensation, benefits, and termination of employment.

I am held responsible for EEO and Affirmative Action performance in this establishment. As President, I have appointed our Human Resources Manager the responsibility to develop and monitor affirmative action and other equal employment opportunity programs. However, management personnel at every level must share in the responsibility for promoting affirmative action and equal employment opportunity to ensure that compliance is achieved.

Harassment of any kind, including sexual harassment, is strictly prohibited. Complaints of harassment will be investigated rapidly and thoroughly and employees who are found to have behaved in such a way will be disciplined, up to possible dismissal from the payroll. Harassment is considered a serious behavior problem and will not be tolerated at XYZ Company. If you have a complaint of harassment, you may see your immediate supervisor, or any management individual, including myself and our Human Resources Manager. You can be assured that we will do all we can to maintain confidentiality, but an investigation will be conducted. Retaliation for filing a complaint of discrimination (of any kind) is not permitted and will not be tolerated.

Equal opportunity must be part of the fabric of all personnel decisions at XYZ Company. Successful performance on our affirmative action goals will provide benefits to the company to the full utilization and development of previously underutilized human resources.

_____

President
1/01/2005

## Notice to Applicants and Employees

XYZ Company maintains affirmative action programs to promote the employment opportunities of disabled individuals, disabled veterans and veterans of the Vietnam era. Employees and applicants may request a review of appropriate portions of the Company's Affirmative Action Program through the human resource department or through their supervisor or department head.

If you are either a disabled individual, a disabled veteran, or a Vietnam era veteran and would like to be considered under these programs, please let your immediate supervisor or department head know. Although giving this information is voluntary, such a disclosure by you will enable the Company to further assist you in an appropriate manner concerning your employment. Be assured that your willingness to provide such information will in no way result in adverse treatment. Information obtained concerning employees will be kept confidential, except that (1) supervisors and department managers may be informed regarding restrictions on the work or duties of disabled employees and disabled veterans and regarding necessary accommodations, and (2) first aid personnel may be informed, when and to the extent appropriate, if a disability might require emergency treatment.

_____
President
1/01/2005

## Equal Employment Opportunity & Affirmative Action Policy

It is the policy of XYZ Company to encourage and support equal employment opportunity for all employees and applicants for employment without regard to sex, race, color, ancestry, religious creed, national origin, physical disability, mental disability, age, marital status, disabled veteran or Vietnam era veteran status. Employment decisions will be evaluated on the basis of an individual's skills, knowledge, abilities, job performance, and other legitimate qualifications, and where appropriate in promotion and transfers, seniority. Equal Employment Opportunity is among the very highest priorities for XYZ Company.

Affirmative action requirements of the federal government are designed to enhance employment opportunities for females and minorities, people with disabilities, disabled veterans, veterans of the Vietnam era, and other eligible veterans. Affirmative action programs provide for fuller utilization and development of all human resources.

Affirmative action and equal employment opportunity affects all employment practices at XYZ Company including recruiting, hiring, transfer, promotion, training, compensation, benefits, and termination of employment.

I am held responsible for EEO and Affirmative Action performance in this establishment. As President, I have appointed our Human Resources Manager the responsibility to develop and monitor affirmative action and other equal employment opportunity programs. However, management personnel at every level must share in the responsibility for promoting affirmative action and equal employment opportunity to ensure that compliance is achieved.

Harassment of any kind, including sexual harassment, is strictly prohibited. Complaints of harassment will be investigated rapidly and thoroughly and employees who are found to have behaved in such a way will be disciplined, up to possible dismissal from the payroll. Harassment is considered a serious behavior problem and will not be tolerated at XYZ Company. If you have a complaint of harassment, you may see your immediate supervisor, or any management individual, including myself and our Human Resources Manager. You can be assured that we will do all we can to maintain confidentiality, but an investigation will be conducted. Retaliation for filing a complaint of discrimination (of any kind) is not permitted and will not be tolerated.

Equal opportunity must be part of the fabric of all personnel decisions at XYZ Company. Successful performance on our affirmative action goals will provide benefits to the company to the full utilization and development of previously underutilized human resources.

_____

President
1/01/2005

## INVITATION TO SELF-IDENTIFY
### For
## DISABLED INDIVIDUALS, DISABLED VETERANS, & VIETNAM ERA VETERANS

XYZ Company is a Government contractor subject to the Vietnam Era Veterans' Readjustment Assistance Act of 1974, as amended, and Section 503 of the Rehabilitation Act of 1973 which require Government contractors to take affirmative action to employ and advance in employment qualified individuals with disability, disabled veterans, veterans of the Vietnam era, and other eligible veterans covered by the Act. If you are an eligible individual with a disability, disabled veteran, veteran of the Vietnam era, or other eligible veteran covered by these acts and would like to be considered under the affirmative action program, please tell us. You may inform us of your desire to benefit under the program at this time and/or at any time in the future. This information will assist us in placing you in an appropriate position and in making accommodations for your disability if you are a disabled person. Submission of this information is voluntary and refusal to provide it will not subject you to any adverse treatment. Information you submit will be kept confidential, except that (a) supervisors and managers may be informed regarding restrictions on the work or duties of disabled individuals, and regarding necessary accommodations; (b) first aid and safety personnel may be informed, when and to the extent appropriate, if the condition might require emergency treatment; and (c) Government officials engaged in enforcing laws administered by OFCCP or the Americans With Disabilities Act, may be informed. The information provided will be used only in ways that are not inconsistent with the *Vietnam Era Veterans' Readjustment Assistance Act of 1974, as amended, the Veterans Employment Opportunities Act, and/or Section 503 of the Rehabilitation Act of 1973.*

I would like to be included in XYZ Company's affirmative action programs qualified individuals with disabilities, and/or special disabled veterans, veterans of the Vietnam era, and other qualified veterans.

| Individual With Disability | Vietnam Veteran |
|---|---|
| Yes _____        No _____ | Yes _____        No _____ |
| Physical Disability:  Yes ___  No ___ | Other Eligible Veteran |
| Mental Disability:   Yes ___  No ___ | Yes _____        No _____ |
| I would like to request the following accommodation: _____<br>_____ | Special Disabled Veteran |
|  | Yes _____        No _____ |

Name: _____Job Title: _____

Signature: _____Date: _____

## Sample Letter
## (On Company Letterhead)

NOTE: This sample can be sent to recruiter agencies, minority groups, women's groups, etc.

1/01/2005

Dear:

Since your organization is a source of referrals for employment opportunities with our company, we wish to take this occasion to restate, in writing, our employment policy. Quoting from that policy: "It is the policy of XYZ Company that there shall be no discrimination on the basis of race, color, religion, sex, age, national origin, disability, marital status, or veteran's status in the hiring or termination of employees; in setting their employment, including opportunities for promotion."

In keeping with the above policy statement, we request that your organization refer qualified applicants to us without regard to race, color, religion, sex, age, national origin, disability, marital status, or veteran's status.

We ask that you retain this letter in your XYZ Company file for future reference. Your assistance and cooperation will be greatly appreciated.

Sincerely,

### Example of "EEO Clause" on Contracts and Purchase Orders

*During the performance of this contract (or purchase order), the contractor/vendor agrees to comply with all Federal, state and local laws respecting discrimination in employment and non-segregation of facilities including, but not limited to, requirements set out at 41 CFR 60—1.4, 60—250.4 and 60—741.4, which equal opportunity clauses are hereby incorporated by reference.*

Some OFCCP compliance officers have been insisting contractors to have an additional obligation with respect to vendors and sub-contractors. There is no regulatory authority for this particular OFCCP demand, however if you do not want to get into an argument with some officer you can include it as well.

*Notification is hereby given that compliance with these clauses may require the contractor/vendor to annually file certain reports (e.g. the EEO-1 Report and the VETS—100 Report) with the Federal government and may require the contractor/vendor to develop written Affirmative Action Programs for Women and Minorities, Covered Veterans and/or Persons with Disabilities.*

# Employment Application Tracking

*To ensure that we maintain proper tracking/records of our employment applications, please complete these forms for each application received and return it to Human Resources. Please note all <u>original</u> applications and resumes must be forwarded and maintained by Human Resources.*

**Position(s) considered for:** _____

_____

## *CIRCLE ONE DISPOSITION CODE*

**Did not interview:**

| | | |
|---|---|---|
| NA | = | Position applied for Not Available/no openings |
| NQ | = | Not Qualified |
| OQ | = | Over Qualified |
| NI | = | Not interested—Other |
| UR | = | Unable to Reach or contact for interview |
| **ID** | **=** | **Interview Declined/No longer interested/found other employment** |
| NSI | = | No Show for Interview |

**Interviewed:**

| | | |
|---|---|---|
| W | = | Applicant withdrew self from further consideration |
| NO | = | Interview conducted—No Offer to be extended |

**Employment Offer:**

| | | |
|---|---|---|
| H | = | Hired |

Position hired for:_____

| | | |
|---|---|---|
| D | = | Declined Offer |
| R | = | Rescinded offer (due to pre-employment screens) |
| NSW | = | No show for work |

Notes: _____
_____
_____
_____
_____

Completed by: _____

Date: _____

**PLEASE RETURN TO HUMAN RESOURCES**

# Compliance Audit Review

## 1. Recruiting and Search Activity

What is your "recruitment area" for the following EEO-1 categories?

| JOB GROUP CATEGORY | EXTERNAL (Where do you advertise?) | INTERNAL (What Job Groups do you look to?) |
|---|---|---|
| Executive/Senior Level Official and Manager | | |
| Mid-Level Official and Manager | | |
| Lower-Level Official and Manager | | |
| Technical Professional (Engineers, Chemists, etc.) | | |
| Non-Technical Professional (Accountants, Human Resources, etc.) | | |
| Technicians | | |
| Sales Workers | | |
| Administrative Support Workers | | |
| Service Workers | | |
| Craft Workers | | |
| Operatives | | |
| Laborers and Helpers | | |

## 2  Recruitment Media

| | |
|---|---|
| | We use the phrase "Equal Opportunity Employer M/F/D/V" in all ads |
| | We use newspapers and other media which are read by minorities |
| | We use newspapers and other media which are read by women |
| | We keep records of responses from ads |
| | We have notified the State Employment Service that XYZ Company is subject to veteran's regulations and listing and reporting requirements thereunder |
| | We list all employment openings that are to be filled by new hires with the local State Employment Service (except jobs in the Executive/senior level, jobs that last 3 days or less, or jobs that were posted internally only |
| | We have minorities and women photographs in employment advertising |
| | We have a policy to define an "employment applicant" |
| | What recruitment agencies do we use? |
| | We have notified these agencies in writing of our being an affirmative action employer (a sample letter is enclosed in the information provided by HR Management Solutions, LLC) |
| | We have records of correspondence with referral sources |

## 3.  Colleges and Schools

| | |
|---|---|
| | We use these schools for recruiting purposes: (also list minority and female population of these, if known) |
| | We have sent letters to these schools (high schools, technical school, colleges): |
| | We have filled these jobs with referrals from these schools: |

## 4. "Word of Mouth" Recruiting

| | |
|---|---|
| | We have a job posting policy |
| | We use "friends and relatives" referrals |
| | We give equal consideration for jobs to friends and relatives of minority and female employees |
| | We encourage minority and female employees to refer relatives and friends |
| | What employees have made referrals of friends or relatives? |

## 5. Walk-Ins

| | |
|---|---|
| | We accept applications for jobs from "walk-ins" (list the jobs you accept "walk-in" apps) |
| | We get a good "walk-in" response from minorities and women |
| | We keep applications for 2 years |

## 6. Special Minority/Female Sources

| | |
|---|---|
| | We use outside organizations (other than recruitment agencies) when we have job openings (list the jobs you have) |
| | We notify outside sources in writing |

## 7. Sources of Disabled Applicants

| | |
|---|---|
| | We have made contacts to organizations for disabled referrals (list those organizations) |
| | Our managers/supervisors are alert that there may be a request for "accommodation" to a disability |

## 8. Veterans

| | |
|---|---|
| | We have made contacts to veterans' organizations for referrals (list) |
| | Managers/supervisors are alert that there may be a request for "accommodation" to a veteran |

## 9. Write-Ins

| | |
|---|---|
| | We accept "unsolicited" resumes as applications (list job titles this applies to) |
| | We send reply letters to write-ins, giving the opportunity for them to "self-identify" |
| | This has been a successful source for us |

## 10. Special Problems

| | |
|---|---|
| | Transportation is adequate from minority areas to our facility |
| | We have a policy on employment of relatives |
| | We offer daycare services for employees |

## 11. Applicant Flow Date on Applicant Log

| | |
|---|---|
| | Is the date of application indicated |
| | Is the applicant's name, apparent race, and sex indicated |
| | Is the position applied for indicated |
| | Is the referral source indicated |
| | Is there an area to indicate if the job was offered |
| | Are individual minority groups applying in proportion to their availability in the area |
| | Are minorities and women applying for positions in jobs where they are underutilized |
| | Are you offering minorities and women jobs in job groups that are underutilized |
| | What are the principal reasons for rejecting applicants |
| | Who makes the final decision to hire and on what basis? |

## 12. Hiring

| | |
|---|---|
| | The employment office is clearly designated and easily located and accessible from the street |
| | The office is "disabled accessible" |
| | The EEO/AA postings are visible to applicants |
| | The people who first see the applicant in the employment office are trained in affirmative action policies and procedures |
| | How are application forms issued |
| | Applicants are interviewed prior to completing an application form |
| | Applicant flow statistics and records are kept current |

## 13. Application Forms

| | |
|---|---|
| | Application forms comply with federal, state, and local laws |
| | The information on the application is entirely job-related |
| | |

Do they conform to federal, state, and local laws?

What is the retention period?

Is your real reason for non-hire listed on the form?

Do you have application forms for minorities and women available for easy retrieval at the time of subsequent job openings?

Is the information on the application form entirely job-related?

What are your rejection ratios for minorities and women?

Do you respond to rejected applicants in writing?

## 14.  Job Descriptions

|  | |
|---|---|
|  | We have written job descriptions or job specifications |
|  | Job descriptions are reviewed periodically to ensure consistency with actual job requirements |
|  | "Trainee" slots are used where appropriate |

## 15.  Job Interviews

|  | |
|---|---|
|  | Interviews are "standardized" where applicants for the same job are asked the same questions |
|  | Adequate and accurate records are kept of the interviews |
|  | Interviews are "rated' |
|  | Has the hiring or interview process ever been challenged?  How? |

## 16.  Testing/Assessments

|  | |
|---|---|
|  | Tests/Assessments are used as a hiring criterion in the selection process |
|  | These tests/assessments conform to the federal Uniform Selection Guidelines |
|  | The person(s) who administer these tests/assessments are trained in correct testing procedures |
|  | The same tests/assessments are used for all (minorities, females, non-minorities, and males) |
|  | Do you have pass/fail rates for minorities, women, non-minorities and men applying for the same job |
|  | These tests/assessments are "weighted" in the hiring decision (how are they "weighted") |
|  | Applicants are notified of their scores on these tests/assessments |

## 17. Placement

| | |
|---|---|
| | We have minorities, women, disabled, and/or disabled veterans interviewers |
| | The following conduct hiring interviews |
| | The EEO coordinator is involved in the hiring process |
| | Who is the final decision-making authority? |
| | Are these decisions reviewed?  By Whom? |
| | Selectors are aware of AAP goals |
| | We have written interview guidelines |
| | We have written evaluation forms and records |

## 18. Job Offers

| | |
|---|---|
| | We keep data and have done an analysis of job offers in the last 12 months |

## 19. Analysis of New Hires

| | |
|---|---|
| | The sources of our new hires: |
| | Women/Minorities are assigned to specific kinds of jobs where there is a high termination rate |

## 20. Advancement

| | |
|---|---|
| | We have an formal appraisal system |
| | The employee participates in the appraisal discussion |
| | We provide counseling and career guidance |
| | We have kept a history of mobility for minorities and women |
| | Job vacancies are communicated as follows: |
| | We offer pre-supervisory and supervisory training |
| | We have a tuition refund program |
| | We have identified training needs for minorities and women in our workforce |
| | We have a formal orientation program |

## 21. Termination

| | |
|---|---|
| | We conduct exit interviews |
| | Our discharge procedures are as follows: |
| | We keep records of minority and women termination ratios |
| | We give out references for terminated employees |
| | We have a complaint procedure for employees who have been disciplined or terminated |

## 22. Layoff and Recall Procedures

| | |
|---|---|
| | We have controls to ensure uniformity in how we apply layoffs and recalls |
| | If seniority is controlling, is plant-wide seniority used as a key factor |

## 23. Auditing Personnel Activities

| | |
|---|---|
| | What follow-up do you have for corrective action when practices are in violation of established policy or government regulations? |

## 24. Dissemination

| | |
|---|---|
| | We have our EEO policy in our policy and procedure manual |
| | We have included a statement of EEO policy in internal XYZ Company publications |
| | Our policy and responsibility has been communicated to upper-level and line management |
| | We have held meetings with employees to discuss our policy and to advise them of our AAP |
| | Our policy is communicated in orientation sessions |
| | We have included articles about minority, female, veteran, and disabled accomplishments and about the Company's EEO efforts within the work force and within the community in Company publications |
| | We have given formal notification to suppliers and subcontractors of XYZ Company's status as a covered employer |
| | We have met with union officials to discuss the Company's affirmative action commitment and sent the formal notice to the union about the Company's EEO responsibilities (if your workforce is organized) |
| | The EEO statement is included in the collective bargaining agreement (if applicable) |

## 25. General

| | |
|---|---|
| | We have reviewed our AAP and responsibilities with line supervision |
| | All EEO posters and policy statements are on employee bulletin boards and wherever employment applications are received |
| | The VETS-100 Report has been filed |
| | We have the last three (3) EEO-1 Reports included in the "Exhibits" portion of our written AAP |
| | We have documented all of our affirmative action activities |
| | We have monitored the progress toward achieving goals |

Are you prepared to explain XYZ Company"s actions and/or progress on the following:

1. Position descriptions—job ratings, pay systems, etc. (can you explain and inconsistencies that may be present?)
2. Testing impact—have you validated or eliminated tests having adverse impact on minorities or females? Are your tests content valid?
3. Accommodations to disabled (e.g., physical/mental requirements, facilities, etc.)
4. Accommodations to employees' religious preferences

# GLOSSARY

**Ability**
A present competence to perform an observable behavior or a behavior which results in an observable product.

**Accessibility**
A disabled individual's ability to approach, enter and use an employer's facilities such as reception areas, employment offices, and the actual job site. Referred to in Section 503 of the Disabled Regulations.

**Administrative Law**
The body of law created by administrative agencies (such as the EEOC and OFCCP) in the form of rules, regulations, orders, and decisions.

**Administrative Law Judge**
A law judge appointed to preside at hearings, including disputes over employment law interpretations.

**Administrative Remedy**
A remedy provided by an administrative agency rather than a court. Before going to court, aggrieved persons are required to pursue and exhaust administrative remedies first. In the equal employment field, administrative remedies include back pay and restoration of the individual to the position he or she would have had, but for the discrimination, or an equivalent position.

## Adverse Impact

The selection of protected-class members at a rate lower than that of other groups. A selection rate for any race, sex, or ethnic group which is less than four-fifths (4/5 or 80%) of the rate for the group with the highest rate will generally be regarded by the enforcement agencies as evidence of adverse impact.

## Affected Class

Employee, former employees, or applicants who have been denied employment opportunities or benefits because of discriminatory practices and/or policies of the employer. Evidence of the existence of an affected class requires identification of the discriminatory practices, identification of the effects of the discrimination, and identification of those suffering from the effects of the discrimination.

## Affirmative Action

Those result-oriented actions which a contractor, by virtue of its contracts, must take to ensure equal employment opportunity. It may include goals to correct underutilization, relief such as back pay, or correction of problem areas. In the area of employment law it refers to concrete steps in hiring or recruitment, transfer, and promotion, or training designed to eliminate the present effects of past discrimination.

## Affirmative Action Clauses

Under the regulations for disabled individuals, disabled veterans, and Vietnam era veterans, affirmative action clauses detail the affirmative action requirements for these protected-class members. The clause is required on all contracts of $10,000 $50,000. Employers with contracts of over $50,000 must also develop affirmative action plans.

## Affirmative Action Plan (AAP)

The "written" plan incorporating a set of specific and results-oriented procedures to which the employer (government contractor) commits itself to apply every good-faith effort to achieve. It is intended to eliminate and remedy past discrimination against or underutilization of minorities and women.

## Affirmative Recruitment

If the utilization analysis shows underutilization of women or minorities in certain job groups, then special recruitment efforts must be mounted to make certain that these protected-class members are well represented in applicant pools for positions which have been historically underutilized. It may include special overt or outreach recruitment efforts at job fairs, special advertising campaigns in minority and women's media, special contacts to organizations which promote placement of minorities and women, etc.

## Age Discrimination in Employment Act (ADEA)
A federal law prohibiting age discrimination by employers of 20 or more employees against people over age 40, except where age is a bona fide occupational qualification or where the person is in a certain key executive or policy-making position and his or her retirement pension will be in excess of $44,000 per year. Such employees may be required to retire at age 65.

## Aggregate Workforce
In the construction industry, it is the total workforce of a covered construction contractor in a certain geographic area as designated by the OFCCP. The definition includes all of the contractor's workforce, including those performing on federally funded or assisted jobs and all nonfederal projects within the designated geographical area.

## Aggrieved Party
A person (or in this case, an employee, former employee, or applicant) whose personal or property rights have been violated by another person.

## American Indian of Alaskan Native
A person with origins in any of the original peoples of North America and who maintains cultural identifications through tribal affiliation or community recognition.

## Annual Goal
Referred to in the goals and timetables section of the affirmative action plan, the annual goal is an annual target (annual in that is the one-year life of the AAP) for placing underutilized groups of protected-class members in those job groups where underutilization exists.

## Anti-nepotism Policy
Employment policies or hiring procedures which may limit the employment of two or more members of the same family.

## Applicant (for federal assistance)
An applicant for federal assistance involving a construction contract, or other participant in a program involving a construction contract, as determined by the regulations of an administrative agency.

## Applicant for Employment
A person seeking work at a company or facility as specified in the employer's policy definition of an employment applicant. It is usually a person, as defined by the employer, who is seeking work at the company and who meets certain prescribed standards as defined by the employer. (For instance, you may limit the definition of "applicant to those who apply for a *specific* job.)

## Applicant Flow
The number of applicants for employment for a given job over a stated period of time, analyzed by sex and minority status.

## Applicant Flow Log
A chronological compilation of applicants for employment or promotion candidates, showing each individuals categorized by race, sex, and ethnic group, who applied for each job title (or group of jobs recruiting similar qualifications) during a specific period.

## Applicant Pool
All people who have applied and met the employer's definition of applicants for particular jobs during AAP plan year or other predetermined period of time. This is the collection of candidates from which the selection of available positions is normally made.

## Apprentice
An employee or new hire who is selected to learn a certain skilled trade in a formal training program which consists of on-the-job training, usually monitored by an experienced craft worker, and related formal instruction at the facility or

in public vocational institutions. This person may be listed or formally indentured with a state apprenticeship committee.

## Arrest and Conviction Records
Records of an employee's arrest for, or conviction of, a crime. Some federal courts have ruled that an employer's practice of disqualifying all applicants with arrest records has an adverse impact on blacks. Such a practice is illegal unless justified by business necessity.

## Asian of Pacific Islander
A person with origins in any of the original peoples of the Far East, Southeast Asia, the Indian subcontinent, or the Pacific Islands. Also included are the countries of China, Japan, Korea, the Philippine Islands, and Samoa. The Indian subcontinent includes: Bangladesh, Bhutan, India, Nepal, Pakistan, Sikkim, and Sri Lanka.

## Availability
Availability figures are determined in a complex availability analysis and are used to determine whether an employer is adequately utilizing minorities and women in specific job groups. Availability means the percentage of available minorities and women with the skills required to perform in a specific job group, or individuals who are capable of acquiring those skills in a short period of time.

Availability percentages are developed for each job group by factoring raw employment statistics with a weighted factor which is designed to consider the employer's particular needs.

## Availability Analysis
See the above definition of *availability*. AKA Eight-Factor Analysis. Under the proposals made to alter 60—2, this will require analysis of only Two Factors, and External and Internal.

## Back Pay
In a conciliation agreement or court order, the EEOC may determine compensation for past losses caused by an employer's discriminatory practices. This may include lost wages, catch-up of fringe benefits, or other pay which is required to

put the person in the position he or she should have had, but for the discrimination.

## Black
A person with origins in any of the black racial groups of Africa who is not of Hispanic origin. Used in determining race codes for EEO and affirmative action plan purposes.

## Bona Fide Occupational Qualification (BFOQ)
Employment in particular jobs may not be limited to individuals of a particular sex, religion, or national origin unless the employer can show that one of these factors is an actual and necessary qualification for performing the job. This concept is interpreted very narrowly by the EEOC. While age may be considered a BFOQ under the Age Discrimination in Employment Act (for public safety workers, airlines pilots, etc.) race is never a BFOQ.

## Burden of Proof
For purposes of definition in this workbook, the term often refers to the burden placed on an employer to present a legitimate, nondiscriminatory reason for its employment action once a member of a protected class shows that he or she has been subject to an adverse employment decision, despite being qualified.

## Business Necessity
Business necessity is justification for an employment practice that would otherwise be considered discriminatory. It is a requirement that is essential to the safe and efficient operation of the business.

## Career Counseling
Sometimes provided by outside professionals or by company employee relations personnel, career counseling considers and develops programs, job transfers, or alternate work experiences which will help the employees advance.

## Career Ladder
A series of steps, job transfers, or promotions through which an employee may advance by furthering the employee's experience, education, and on-the-job training.

### Census Bureau (U.S. Bureau of the Census)
This agency conducts the 10-year census of the population. The agency's compilation of this data is generally regarded as acceptable data for contents of an affirmative action plan. The bureau is part of the federal Department of Commerce.

### Charging Party
A person who charges that he or she has been discriminated against in violation of one of the federal employment discrimination statutes. In some state jurisdictions, the person is then called the plaintiff.

### Chilling Effect
Any practice which has the effect of seriously discouraging the exercise of a right.

### Civilian Labor Force
The total of people at work, as determined by the U.S. Bureau of the Census at a given point in time. The term includes both employed and unemployed people. Requisite skills is not considered in this pool.

### Civil Rights
The right of certain individuals not to be discriminated against in employment, public accommodations, housing, voting, and education because of their protected-class status.

### Civil Rights Act of 1964
The nation's first comprehensive law making it illegal to discriminate on the basis of race, color, religion, sex, and national origin. Title VII of that law, which is enforced by the Equal Employment Opportunity Commission, is specifically aimed at discrimination in employment.

### Class Action
Occurs if the regional or Washington office of the EEOC concludes that a complaint of discrimination against other employees of similar characteristics in the organization, and the EEOC files a suit in federal court on behalf of the entire affected class.

## Code of Federal Regulations (CFR)
Federal statutes and executive orders are broad, general statements of law. Federal regulation, on the other hand, fill in the details. For example, Executive Order 11246 requires federal contractors to take affirmative action. The federal regulations issued under that executive order specify exactly how the contractor should do that. This workbook explains those federal regulations.

## Collective Bargaining Agreement
A "written" contract between an employer and a labor union, for a definitive period of time, spelling out conditions of employment, wages, hours of work, rights of employees and the union, and procedures to be followed in settling disputes.

## Compliance
Meeting the requirements and obligations imposed by Executive Order 11246, as amended, Section 503 of the Rehabilitation Act of 1973, as amended, or 38 U.S.C. §4212 and their implementing regulations..

## Concentration
More females or minorities in a job group than their relative proportion in the labor market workforce.

## Conciliation
The process of negotiation to correct findings of noncompliance which is aimed at reaching a settlement agreeable to both parties. This is the first step the EEOC takes when it finds reasonable cause to believe that discrimination has taken place. The object of conciliation is to find relief for the person(s) affected.

## Conciliation Agreement
A "written" agreement between an employer and a state or federal anti-discrimination agency that details specific contractor commitments to resolve identified compliance deficiencies which are set forth in the agreement.

## Construction Contract
Any contract for the construction, rehabilitation, alteration, conversion, extension, demolition, or repair of buildings or highways, or other changes or improvements to real property.

## Contract
Any "Government contract" or "subcontract," or for the Executive Order, any "Federally assisted construction contract or subcontract."

## Contracting Agency
Any department, agency, or branch of the government, including any wholly owned government corporation, which enters into contracts.

## Contractor
A prime contractor or subcontractor to the federal government.

## Corporate Management Compliance Evaluations
A revision that would permit the scope of a Corporate Management Compliance Evaluation (glass ceiling review) to extend beyond corporate headquarters, when OFCCP becomes aware that compliance problems exist at other corporate locations. In this way, nationwide systemic pay discrimination could be corrected.

## Corrective Action
Correction of deficiencies identified during a compliance review of an affirmative action plan. The term is used in deficiency letters, conciliation agreements, and show-cause orders.

## Debarment
A sanction which disqualifies a company from bidding of future government contracts or subcontracts and which may terminate current contracts or subcontracts.

## Deficiency
Noncompliance with any government regulation.

## Department of Labor (DOL)
The administrative agency of the federal government which enforces and administers laws and regulations affecting employees at work.

### Desk Audit
A review and analysis at the desk of the Equal Opportunity Specialist in the Department of Labor offices which determines the acceptability of the employer's affirmative action plans under the regulations.

### Disabled Individual
Any person who (1) has a physical or mental disability that substantially limits one or more of his or her major life activities, (2) has a record of such disability, or (3) is regarded as having such disability. A disability is substantially limiting if it is likely to cause difficulty in securing, or advancing in employment.

### Disabled Veteran
A person entitled to compensation under laws administered by the Veterans Administration for disability rated at 30% or more, or a person whose discharge or release from active duty was for a disability incurred or aggravated in the line of duty.

### Discrimination
Illegal treatment of a person or group based on race, sex, or other prohibited factor. There are two types of discrimination: disparate treatment and disparate impact. Disparate treatment means treating a person differently because of his or her race, sex, disability, or other protected-class status. Disparate impact, a less blatant form of discrimination, means a practice which has a greater negative effect on members of protected-classes than on others.

### Disparate Impact
The likelihood that a test, job qualification, or other employment practice will screen out or otherwise limit the employment opportunities of minorities, or women, or other protected-class members at a greater rate than others.

### Disparate Treatment
A theory or category of employment discrimination. Disparate impact discrimination may be found when a contractor's use of a facially neutral selection standard (e.g., a test, an interview, a degree requirement) disqualifies members of a particular race or gender group at a significantly higher rate than others and is not justified by business necessity or job-relatedness. An intent to discriminate is not necessary to this type of employment discrimination.

**"Dun's Number" (D & B)**
A special number assigned to a business entity by Dun and Bradstreet Co., a financial reporting organization, for computer identification of that company or local unit. Also known as "D & B."

**EEO-1 Category or Code**
The nine broad job categories used on the EEO-1 Report. These are Officials and Managers, Professionals, Technicians, Sales Workers, Office and Clerical, Craft Workers, Operatives, Laborers, and Service Workers.

**EEO-1 Report**
The annual Equal Opportunity Employer Information Report filed by "government contractors" with the federal government. Also known as the Standard Form 100, the report details the race, ethnic, and sex composition of the employer's workforce by sex category at the start of the calendar year or other time period from January 1-September 30 in year.

**"Eighty Percent" Rule**
The "rule of thumb" for determining adverse impact. A selection rate for any group which is less than 80% (four-fifths) of the rate for other groups is evidence of violation of this rule.

**Employer**
For purposes of definition in this workbook, any employer subject to the provisions of the Civil Rights Act of 1964, as amended, including state or local governments; any federal agency subject to the provisions of Section 717 of the Civil Rights Act, as amended; and any federal contractor or subcontractor or federally assisted construction contractor covered by Executive Order 11246, as amended. (See discussion of specific laws for detailed coverage information.)

**Employment Agency**
Any employment agency subject to the provisions of the Civil Rights Act of 1964 as amended, for purposes of definition in this workbook. It means any person(s) regularly undertaking, with or without compensation, procurement of employees for an employer or procurement for employees of opportunities to work for an employer, and includes an agent of such person(s).

**Employment Offer**
An employer's offer to an applicant for employment, usually in a specific job.

**Employment Practice**
Any recruitment, hiring, selection practice, any transfer or promotion policy, or any benefit provision or other function of the employer's employment process which operates as an analysis or screening device.

**Enforcement**
Using legal means to enforce compliance.

**Enforcement Action**
A proceeding by a federal enforcement agency to make sure that the law is being followed. In the case of affirmative action, enforcement could range from a simple desk audit to the investigation of a discrimination complaint. Enforcement action could ultimately result in termination of federal government contracts.

**Equal Employment Opportunity (EEO)**
A system of employment practices under which no individuals are excluded from consideration, participation, promotion, or benefits because of their race, color, religion, sex, national origin, age, disability, or veteran status. The purpose of affirmative action is to achieve equal employment opportunity.

**Equal Employment Opportunity Commission (EEOC)**
The federal government agency designated to enforce Title VII of the Civil Rights Act of 1964, the Equal Pay Act of 1963, and the Age Discrimination in Employment Act of 1967. The Commission has five members, all appointed to a five-year term by the president with the advice and approval of Congress.

**Equal Opportunity Clause**
The seven subparagraphs contained in Section 202 of Executive Order 11246, as amended, and required to be part of all contracts covered by the executive order.

**Equal Opportunity Specialist (EOS)**
An employee of the federal Department of Labor charged with the responsibility of interviewing and processing employment discrimination charges or conducting compliance reviews of employers' affirmative action programs.

## Equal Opportunity Survey
This proposal would require a substantial number of contractors to submit this Survey each year. The EO Survey would collect information on a contractor's Federal government contracts and affirmative action programs, personnel activity and compensation data. The EO Survey would also assist contractors in conducting self-evaluation and therebvy facilitate voluntary compliance.

## Equal Pay Act of 1963
A federal law which required equal pay between the sexes on jobs that are equal in skill, effort, and responsibility.

## Establishment
A facility or unit which produces goods or services, such as a factory, office, store, or mine. In most instances, the unit is a physically separate facility at a single location. In appropriate circumstances, OFCCP may consider as an establishment several facilities located at two or more sites when the facilities are in the same labor market or recruiting area. The determination as to whether it is appropriate to group facilities as a single establishment will be made by OFCCP on a case-by-case basis.

## Ethnic Group
A group identified on the basis of religion, color, or national origin.

## Executive Order
A regulation promulgated by the president which has the effect of law on those governmental matters with which it deals.

## Executive Orders 11246, 11375, and 12086
These orders require federal contractors with contracts of $10,000 or more to agree to grant equal employment opportunity on the basis of race, color, religion, sex, and national origin. Additionally, the orders require those who employ 50 or more employees and who hold contracts of $50,000 or more to develop "written" affirmative action plans.

## Executive Order 11701

Promulgated in 1973, the order authorizes the secretary of labor to issue regulations requiring federal agencies to list their jobs openings with state employment services.

## Exempt Positions

Generally managerial, supervisory, and professional types of positions which are exempt from the overtime provisions of the federal Fair Labor Standards Act.

## Facially Neutral Selection Standards/Criteria

A criterion/process is facially neutral if it does not make any reference to a prohibited factor and is equally applicable to everyone regardless of race, gender, or ethnicity, i.e., is not discriminatory on its face.

## Fair Employment Practices Agency (FEPA)

A state of local government agency which administers state or local laws, regulations, or ordinances prohibiting employment discrimination on the basis of sex, minority status, and other prohibited factors. Sometimes called the fair housing and employment agency or the state human relations commission where jurisdictions go beyond the employment scene.

## Federally Assisted Construction Contract

All construction projects for which the federal government itself contracts directly, or which the federal government guarantees or insures, such as housing insured by the Federal Housing Administration.

## Focus Job

A job title, department, or seniority unit of the employer's workforce in which minorities or women are concentrated or underrepresented in comparison to their availability for the jobs or in the workforce itself.

## Fringe Benefits

Those elements of employment compensation over and above basic wages or salary such as life insurance, medical and hospital benefits, pension or retirement benefits, sick leave, and vacation and holiday pay.

## Goal Achievement
An employer's meeting of its employment or promotion targets set to correct the underutilization of protected-class members.

## Goals
An employer's annual percentage rate of selection or internal promotion in areas of underutilization, which are to be achieved through good-faith effort.

## Goals and Timetables (G and T)
An employer who underutilizes women or minorities is required to make numerical projections of good-faith efforts to hire or promote these protected classes. These are called goals. The current timetable framework for affirmative action plans is a one-year period. Goals and timetables are not quotas.

## Good Cause
A legally acceptable defense for not having taken action that would otherwise be required. Good cause for a violation of 41 CFR Chapter 60 can normally be demonstrated only by showing that a firm is or was not covered by the regulation allegedly violated, or is exempt from the regulation.

## Good-Faith Efforts
Those actions that the contractor may voluntarily develop to achieve compliance with the contact's equal opportunity and affirmative action clauses. The results of these efforts are measured by the contractor's degree of adherence to goals and timetables. Good-faith efforts may excuse a contractor from failing to meet a goal or save the employer from sanctions.

## Government Contract
An agreement or modification thereof between a contracting agency and any person or firm for the furnishing of supplies or services, or for the use of real personal property, including lease arrangements.

## Griggs v. Duke Power Co.
The landmark U.S. Supreme Court decision of 1971 which determined that employment tests or qualifications which screen out minorities or women at a higher rate than other candidates cannot be used unless the employer proves that

such a selection method is related to the job for which it is used. Such proof must be in the form of a validation study.

## Hispanic
A person of Mexican, Puerto Rican, Cuban, South American, or other Spanish culture or origin, regardless of race.

## Immigration Reform and Control Act of 1986
This Act makes it unlawful for virtually all U.S. employers and referral agencies to employ or recruit for a fee aliens not authorized to work in the United States. It requires employers to verify the right of each applicant to work in this country.

## Impact Ratio
For employment decisions which offer people employment opportunities (e.g., hiring, promotion, training), the impact ratio for a group is the selection rate for the group of people in question divided by the selection rate for the group with the highest selection rate. For any adverse employment decision (e.g., termination, disciplinary action, layoff) the impact ratio is the (termination) rate of the group with the lowest rate divided by the (termination) rate for the group in question. Impact ratios are compared to the 80% "rule of thumb" to determine if adverse impact exists.

## Internal Review Procedure
A procedure by which an employer can adequately address and resolve a complaint of employment discrimination made by a disabled individual, a disabled veteran, or a Vietnam era veteran. Federal regulations permit employers first to use their own review procedures to handle complaints by disabled people or veterans. Complaints that allege discrimination or affirmative action violations on account of race, religion, sex, or national origin are filed directly with the federal government. In these situations there is no opportunity for the employer initially to use its own review procedures.

## Invitation to Self-Identify
An invitation by an employer extended to all employees and applicants who believe they are covered by Section 402 or 503 to identify themselves as disabled, disabled veterans, or Vietnam era veterans for purposes of making reasonable

accommodation and taking affirmative action on their behalf. All information obtained in response to such and invitation is to be kept confidential.

## Job Categories
See the definition of *EEO-1 category or code*

## Job Description
A "written" statement detailing the responsibilities and duties of incumbents in a particular job title.

## Job Group
One or more positions having similar content, wage rates, and opportunities.

## Job Qualifications
The education, work experience, and other abilities required for a job.

## Joint Reporting Committee
The EEO-1 Report was jointly developed by the EEOC and the OFCCP, and the Joint Reporting Committee implements those reporting requirements.

## Labor Force
All persons in the civilian labor force, plus members of the armed forces.

## Labor Force Participation
The rate at which a given group (usually referring to protected-class groups) is represented in the civilian labor force.

## Labor Organization
Any labor organization, for purposes of definition in this workbook, subject to the provisions of the Civil Rights Act of 1964, and any committee subject thereto which controls apprenticeship or training.

## Layoff
The process by which active workers are removed from the active payroll to the inactive payroll due to a reduction in workforce.

## Life Activities
Those activities which may be limited by an individual's disability. They include communication, ambulation, self-care, socialization, evaluation, vocational training, employment, transportation, and adaption to housing.

## Line of Progression
The order of jobs in the line through which an employee moves to reach the top of the line.

## Mediation
The process of settling a disagreement between two parties. For purposes of definition in this workbook the term frequently refers to the efforts of an EEO counselor to facilitate resolution of a dispute involving an EEO complaint.

## Metropolitan Statistical Area (MSA)
Any place of 50,000 or more population within an area of 100,000 or more population, or a county or group of contiguous counties which contains at least one city of 50,000 inhabitants or more, or "twin cities" within a combined population of 50,000 or more. Formerly called Standard Metropolitan Statistical Area (SMSA).

## Minorities
All persons classified as black (not of Hispanic origin), Hispanic, Asian or Pacific Islander, or American Indian or Alaskan Native.

## Modification
Any alterations in the terms and conditions of a contract, including supplemental agreements, amendments, and extensions.

## National Alliance of Business (NAB)
A private association supported by business organizations, with some government funding, that works primarily to upgrade minorities for employment opportunities through training and other programs.

## National Association for the Advancement of Colored People (NAACP)
A private association that works to eliminate racial discrimination in all aspects of the social, economic, and political life in the United States.

## National Origin
This term refers not only to one's place of birth, but to an ancestor's place of birth as well.

## New Hire
An employee added to the employer's payroll for the first time.

## Noncompliance
This is the failure to follow the conditions specified in a contract's equal opportunity or affirmative action clauses and the regulations applicable to those clauses.

## Nondiscrimination
The absence of either overt or intentional discrimination, or discrimination resulting from actions that have greater adverse impact on a protected class.

## Nondiscrimination Clause
A clause required in federal contracts with suppliers in which the supplier commits to take affirmative action in employment, upgrading, transfer, promotion, demotion, layoff, termination, and training.

## Notices to be Posted
Notices to employees, applicants for employment, and union members prepared and approved by the Equal Employment Opportunity Commission which described pertinent provisions of the law or regulations, and information pertaining to the filing of a complaint.

## Office of Federal Contract Compliance Programs (OFCCP)
An office within the U.S. Department of Labor which has the responsibility of administering Executive Order 11246 and its implementing regulations.

## On-site
Taking place at the employer's facility.

## On-the-Job Training
The process of learning a job by actually performing it under close supervision or with assistance.

## Organizational Profile
This revision proposes to replace the workforce analysis required by current Section 60—2.11. The proposed organizational profile is a shorter, simpler format, which in most cases would be based upon the contractor's existing organizational chart(s).

## Organizational Unit
A group of closely related jobs or function (for example, a department, branch, or section) which functions as a single unit.

## Parity
For purposes of definition in this workbook, the employment of women and minorities in various job groups at levels which approximate the external availability of qualified members of those groups for those particular job categories.

Pattern or Practice Discrimination
Employer actions constituting a pattern of conduct resulting in discriminatory treatment toward the members of a class.

## Physical and Mental Job Qualifications
Standards set by employers to determine an applicant's ability to perform a job.

## Placement Goal
Serves as an objective that is reasonably attainable by means of applying every good faith effort to make all aspects of the affirmative action program work. Placement Goals are established for Job Groups in which incumbency is deemed to be below the actual expected based on the application of one of the analytical calculations. The Placement Goal, if required, would at least equal the availability for that particular group in the recruitment area.

## Pre-employment Medical Examination
Evaluation of the health status of applicants for employment by company-designated medical personnel.

## Pregnancy Disability
The period during which a female employee is unable to do the duties of the job because of pregnancy, childbirth, or related medical conditions. Employees in

this situation must be treated the same as those with disabilities case by other medical conditions.

## Privacy Act
Protects against unauthorized use of personally identified data by any agency of the federal government. The employees must consent to the release of the data.

## Promotion
A personnel action which results in a person moving to a job requiring higher skill or talents and usually involving greater pay or title.

## Protected Class
A group of people protected from employment discrimination under government regulations and laws, specifically identified as women, blacks, Hispanics, Asians or Pacific Islander, American Indians or Alaskan Natives, people of age 40, the disabled as defined under Section 503, and disabled veterans and Vietnam era veterans.

## Qualified Disabled Veteran
A disabled veteran who is capable of performing a particular job with reasonable accommodation to his or her disability.

## Qualified Disabled Individual
A disabled individual who is capable of performing a particular job with reasonable accommodation to his or her disability.

## Race
A division of humankind having certain common distinguishing physical characteristics that indicate origination in a distinct primitive source.

## Reasonable Accommodation
Changes in the job or workplace which enable a disabled individual or disable veteran to perform the work. Also refers to adjustments make by an employer to accommodate an employee whose religious beliefs forbid working certain days and hours.

### Reasonable Cause
An EEOC determination that there is a basis to believe that a charge or complaint is true.

### Reasonable Commuting Area
The area from which employees can reasonably be expected to commute to an employer's workplace.

### Recruiting Area
The area from which an employer can and does expect to recruit employees.

### Reduction in Force (RIF)
A term used for layoff, frequently so used in the federal government.

### Regarded as Disabled
An individual treated or regarded by the employer as disabled but who may either have no physical or mental impairment, or have an impairment that does not limit his or her major life activities.

### Rehabilitation Act of 1973
A federal law that requires contractors and subcontractors with contracts in excess of $2,500 to take affirmative action to employ and advance in employment disabled individuals.

### Rehired Employee
An employee returned to the payroll after a period of layoff or a break in continuous service

### Relevant Labor Area
The labor market area from which candidates are usually drawn for certain jobs. This may be a local area (secretaries and general plant help) or a national market for such positions as outside salespersons, executives and managers, or even certain professionals.

### Religion
Includes all aspects of religious observance and practice as well as belief.

### Remedies
The means used to correct problem areas; a term used in conciliation agreements and letters of commitment. The purpose of the remedial provisions of the Civil Rights Act is to make whole the victims of discrimination.

### Requisite Skills
The skills needed to do a job; those skills that make a person eligible for consideration for employment in a job.

### Respondent
An employer, labor union, or employment agency charged in having discriminated in violation of a federal or state employment-related law.

### Revised Order No. 4
The regulation promulgated by the U.S. Department of Labor describing the required contents of affirmative action plans.

### Sanctions
Restrictions placed on a contractor who is found to be in noncompliance.

### Segregated Facilities
Facilities belonging to an employer which provide different accommodations for members of one race than those of another. Although the language of Title VII provides that segregation on the basis of sex is prohibited, separate lavatory, locker, shower, and other personal facilities have not been declared unlawful.

### Selection Procedures
Any measures or procedures used as the basis for an employment decision. Selection procedures range from traditional paper-and-pencil tests, performance tests, training programs, probationary periods, and physical, educational, and work experience requirements. They also may include informal or casual interviews and answers on application forms.

### Selection Rate
The proportion of applicants or candidates who are hired, promoted, or otherwise selected.

**Seniority**
A term used to designate an employee's starting date with the company or within a particular organizational unit of the company or to designate an employee's status relative to other employees.

**Sex Discrimination**
Discriminatory or disparate treatment of an individual because of his or her sex.

**Show-Cause Order**
A letter to a federal contractor showing that it has 30 days to show "good cause" why administrative proceedings should not be instituted for its failure to submit an acceptable affirmative action plan within 30 days, or because its plan deviates substantially from an acceptable plan.

**Standard Industrial Classification (SIC) Code**
A numerical identification for various types of industries, developed and published by the Office of Management and Budget. The SIC code classifies employers according to the products or services they make or provide.

**Statistically Significant**
A number of persons, or a mathematically significant quantity, that is large enough to allow a judgement to be made based on statistical analysis.

**Subcontract**
Any agreement or arrangement between a contractor and any person for the furnishing of supplies or services or for the use of real or personal property.

**Subcontractor**
Any person holding a subcontract.

**Substantially Limits**
The effect of a disability on an individual's employability to such a degree that he or she is likely to have difficulty in securing, retaining, or advancing in employment.

**Systemic Discrimination**
Employment policies or practices which, though may appear neutral, serve to differentiate or perpetuate a differentiation in terms or conditions of employ-

ment of applicants or employees because of their race, color, religion, sex, national origin, disability, or veteran status. Systemic discrimination usually refers to a recurring practice rather than to an isolated act of discrimination and may include failure to remedy the effects of past discrimination.

## Technical Deficiency
A minor deficiency in an affirmative action plan such as failure to display the EEO poster, failure to obtain the signature of the location manager on an affirmative action plan, etc.

## Title VII
A federal law that prohibits discrimination in employment on the basis of race, color, religion, sex, or national origin. It applies to all employers of 15 or more employees, regardless of whether or not they are federal contractors.

## Transfer
Movement from one position or another, usually lateral in terms of responsibilities and usually without an increase in compensation.

## Underrepresentation
Fewer women or minorities in a job group than their proportion in the contractor's workforce.

## Underutilization
Having fewer women or minorities in the employer's workforce than could reasonably be expected based on their availability in the labor area.

## Undue Hardship
In order for an employer to be able to refuse an employee's request for accommodation because of disability or religious beliefs, the employer must be able to prove that the accommodation would cause undue hardship. Undue hardship is measured in terms of business necessity and financial cost and expenses.

## Uniform Guidelines on Employee Selection Procedures (USG)
Regulations which set forth the standards by which the federal government determines the acceptability of employee selection procedures. Also known as *Uniform Selection Guidelines.*

**Unlawful Employment Practice**
Any policy, practice, or procedure which tends to discriminate.

**Utilization Analysis**
The comparison of the number of minorities and women in the employer's workforce and the jobs that they occupy, to the availability of minorities and women in the contractor's labor area, and, in the case of promotional jobs, those promotable employees in the contractor's own workforce.

**Validation**
A procedure by which an employer's selection methods are demonstrated to be predictive of job performance. Selection procedures or selection devices which screen out minorities or women at a greater rate than other people must be validated according to procedures under the Uniform Selection Guidelines.

**Vietnam Era Veteran**
A person who served on active duty for a period of more that 180 days, any part of which occurred between August 5, 1964 and May 7, 1975, and was discharged or released therefrom with other than a dishonorable discharge, or was discharged or released from active duty for a service-connected disability if any part of such duty was between the above-listed dates and who was so discharged or released within 48 months preceding the alleged violation of the Vietnam Era Veterans Readjustment Act of 1974.

**Vietnam Era Veterans Readjustment Act of 1974**
A federal law that requires firms holding federal contracts or subcontracts of $10,000 or more to take affirmative action to hire and advance in employment disabled veterans and Vietnam era veterans.

**White**
A person with origins in any of the original peoples of Europe, North Africa, or the Middle East who is not of Hispanic Origin.

### Word-of-Mouth Recruitment
Relying on present employees as a means of securing new applicants for employment.

### Workforce
The total number of workers actively employed in a company.

### Workforce Analysis
A listing of each job title as it appears in the applicable collective bargaining agreement or payroll records, ranked from lowest to highest paid within each department or other similar organizational unit, including department or unit supervision.

0-595-33663-9